HERITAGE HALL

Biography
of a Building

MARIAN GILMOUR
& GAIL BUENTE

DEDICATED TO the volunteer
members of the National Association
of Watch and Clock Collectors,
Chapter 121. Thanks for taking such
fine care of the Heritage Hall clock.

RUSSIAN & U
RESTAURA

ROBIN WARD ILLUSTRATION, FROM *ROBIN WARD'S VANCOUVER*, HARBOUR PUBLISHING

Heritage Hall Preservation Society
Mezzanine, 3102 Main Street
Vancouver, British Columbia
Canada V5T 3G7
www.heritagehall.bc.ca

WRITERS Gail Buente, Marian Gilmour and Ellen Schultz
EDITOR Marian Gilmour
PHOTO EDITOR Gail Buente
DESIGN AND PRODUCTION Elaine Littmann
PRINCIPAL PHOTOGRAPHER Douglas Kennedy
PHOTO SCANNING Leslie Field
PROJECT ADVISORS Catherine Edwards and Cynthia Crampton
CHAPTER TITLE PAGE PHOTOS Douglas Kennedy

Printed and bound in Canada by Webcom

National Library of Canada Cataloguing in Publication Data

Gilmour, Marian.
  Heritage Hall, biography of a building

  ISBN 0-9730138-0-X

  1. Heritage Hall (Vancouver, B.C.) 2. Historic buildings—British Columbia—
Vancouver. I. Buente, Gail. II. Heritage Hall Preservation Society. III. Title.
FC3847.8.H47G54 2002   971.1'33   C2002-910345-2
F1089.5.V22G54 2002

Published with the financial assistance of
British Columbia 2000, Marking The Millennium.

Introduction

Its weathered stones, ornate exterior decoration and towering clock provide a physical link to our collective past.

People love to speculate about the big brown carved stone and brick building with the clock tower at the corner of Main and 15th Avenue. Some think it was an early city hall; others visualize a church; some think it was a bank. One little neighbourhood boy is sure it is a castle. Those in the know call it the old Post Office or the old RCMP building.

Opened in 1916, the building has been a part of day-to-day life in the neighbourhood for several generations. As a federal government building, it served the citizens of Vancouver for six decades. At the end of that cycle it was looking tired and somewhat neglected and its future was not a sure thing. It exists in 2002 because citizens and public servants realized the importance of maintaining this building of character as part of our heritage.

But preserving an outstanding building is of little value unless that building has a useful purpose. These same citizens worked together to find an exciting new function for the building. The idea of converting the upper floors for office space for non-profit community agencies and the eventual decision to use the grand main floor room as a cultural and community facility was a good one. But that doesn't mean it was all smooth sailing.

I have had the privilege of working as the Heritage Hall building manager for the last seven years. It takes me nine minutes to walk to work each day. My house is located half-way up Little Mountain and I get a good view of the neighbourhood from my third floor bedroom window. Each morning when I open my blinds, I can see the building's steep red roof, clock tower, and flag pole. Each morning I am glad to see the building is still there. It stands as a grand lone messenger from a different era in Vancouver's history. Its weathered stones, ornate exterior decoration and towering clock provide a physical link to our collective past. In some ways it has become a touchstone for the community.

People often drop by the building just to look around and reminisce. One older fellow comes every two or three years to reflect on his childhood in the neighbourhood, to recall the soccer fields and the creeks, and the bustle of Main Street. Others come to talk about the ice cream counter at the local dairy and the city car barns that now exist only in memory. Sometimes visitors will pass along an account of a ghost in the building, or the frequently told tale that the original plans were intended for an entirely different building in another city.

The number of people with either an old or relatively new connection to the building is vast. When planning this book I put out a public call for stories about the building. I heard from, among others, a man whose grandfather was a caretaker here in the very early years, a woman who remembers the building as the neighbourhood "palace" and who recalls buying stamps here as a little girl, a man who registered here for the military during WWII, and from a long-retired veterinarian from the Department of Agriculture which had administrative offices here.

In the last two decades hundreds of people have been married here, others have enjoyed birthdays, anniversaries, bar mitzvahs, celebrations and gatherings of all sorts. And even those without a connection seem curious and interested. Many people profess love for the structure. I am one of them.

The building embodies the spirit of a past age of optimism, of high hopes and big dreams. Its very existence is also testament to the hopes and dreams, as well as the hard work, of the dedicated people who rescued and restored it for the future. The story of this building is the story of the neighbourhood and the city itself.

This history of Heritage Hall is an attempt to give life to some of the shadowy, invisible things that have happened here in the last 85 years. The content consists of selected oral history and researched documentation.

Marian Gilmour

Its very existence is testament to the hopes, dreams, and hard work of the dedicated people who rescued and restored it for future use.

7

CHAPTER ONE

The Early Years

MOUNT PLEASANT: UPTOWN VANCOUVER

In the 1880s and 1890s, the early days of Vancouver, everything happened "Downtown," that is, either in Gastown or along a short stretch of Hastings Street. The area we know as Mount Pleasant was at first rather remote, notable mainly for being a stop along the road that led to New Westminster.

But it wasn't long after Vancouver's incorporation as a city in 1886 that people began moving to the suburbs, which in those days meant moving "Uptown", to the area south of False Creek, up the hill on Westminster Avenue (Main Street), to a sparsely populated neighbourhood between 9th Avenue and 16th Avenue, the boundary with the municipality of South Vancouver.

As the neighbourhood began to grow, it started to acquire a sense of its own identity. An article in the *Daily News-Advertiser* of July 10, 1888 stated, "The residents of the Fifth Ward, who are tired of hearing their charming portion of the city spoken of as 'across False Creek', have been casting about for some time for a fitting designation for that lovely suburb, and the other day a lady suggested it should be called Mount

As the neighbourhood began to grow, it started to acquire a sense of its own identity.

8

Pleasant. It is likely that the name will be adopted and a ratification meeting held shortly, to solemnly christen it."

Still, a late 19th century suburb in no way resembled a suburb of today. Along with tidy bungalows on small lots, there was still room enough for orchards and dairy farms. Huge wild areas of underbrush and tree stumps filled the spaces between elegant new frame homes. The streets were unpaved and sidewalks, where they existed, were made of plank. False Creek extended over to about where Clark Drive is now, with numerous streams feeding into it. Trout and salmon swam in Mackie, Fibson, and China Creek, and Brewery Creek, which crossed over Westminster Avenue in several places. In the summertime, residents out for an evening stroll sometimes encountered deer, beavers and even the occasional black bear in the wooded portions of the area. In winter, the ground was often so wet that a stroll was out of the question.

In his memoirs of those years, early Vancouver resident William Pleming recalled: "It was February, 1890. The depressions in the various parts of South Vancouver were filled with water, the natural exits blocked by beaver dams or debris. The stretch of land from Fraser Street to Westminster Avenue along 15th Avenue was one such place. I had occasion to go out that way at this time. When hiring the horse and buggy from McDonald's livery stable on Cordova Street, he enquired if I had been out that way before. 'No,' I replied, 'I have not been very long

Huge wild areas of underbrush and tree stumps filled the spaces between elegant new frame homes.

9

A panoramic view of turn-of-the-century Mount Pleasant taken from Broadway between Main and Quebec Streets.
CITY OF VANCOUVER ARCHIVES PHOTOS

Mount Pleasant was well on its way to being Vancouver's most popular residential area.

Uptown residents wait to hop a streetcar at 9th Avenue and Westminster Avenue, circa 1905.
VANCOUVER PUBLIC LIBRARY PHOTO

in Vancouver.' 'Well,' he said, 'You go up Mount Pleasant and follow the Westminster Road [now Kingsway] to the junction, then bear away to the right and follow the road to the river. You will find a soft spot in the road as you leave the junction, but if you get stuck, remember we get a dry time here about August!'"

In 1891 the journey "Uptown" got a little bit easier when the streetcars began to run along Westminster Avenue to 9th Avenue. The neighbourhood became the favourite housing district for workers from the sawmills edging False Creek.

The public took to streetcars with enthusiasm. Now people could go anywhere with ease: to work, out to the opera, or visiting friends in another neighbourhood, and all for a nickel. In short, streetcars made it possible for anyone to live comfortably in the suburbs.

William Pleming remembered that as well. "Mount Pleasant was emerging from its stumps and becoming quite popular as a residential district. It was joined to Vancouver by a shaky bridge. I was working in the B.C. Electric Railway Shops. A man came in quite excited, and said 'There's a car gone over Westminster Avenue Bridge with 20 people in it.' 'Anybody drowned?' I cried, remembering a similar streetcar tragedy in Victoria. 'Why, no,' he said, 'It just crossed the bridge and has gone up

the hill alright.' Quite relieved, I queried, 'Well, what of it?' 'Oh,' he said, 'it shows how Mount Pleasant is growing, doesn't it?'"

Mount Pleasant was well on its way to being Vancouver's most popular residential area, as well as the location of many light industries and commercial enterprises. The numerous freshwater streams attracted no less than five breweries to the neighbourhood. Two slaughterhouses and a tannery also established themselves in the area. The local school had to be expanded several times to accommodate the influx of families. Churches of various

The arrival of the streetcar lines in 1891 gave the neighbourhood a welcome boost.
BREWERY CREEK HISTORICAL SOCIETY PHOTO

denominations moved into the area. The neighbourhood even had its own uniformed band, and a permanent bandstand. As the population grew, drygoods retailers, druggists, greengrocers, and bakeries sprang up at all the major intersections. Streetcar routes were extended to the South Vancouver boundary at 16th Avenue, and a new terminus was built at 13th and Westminster Avenue.

By 1910, everyone was convinced of the radiant future of Mount Pleasant, so much so that in July of that year, city council passed Bylaw # 739 changing the name of its most important artery, Westminster Avenue, to the more auspicious Main Street. The previous year, 9th Avenue had been rechristened Broadway, in hopes that the area would become the heart of a metropolis as grand as New York City. Uptown was on its way up, or so it seemed.

For a variety of reasons however, these changes never came to be. Vancouver's growth slowed and shifted west to Granville Street and beyond. In hindsight, the extravagant predictions for Mount Pleasant might seem slightly preposterous, but the climate at the time encouraged such thinking.

THE GOLDEN YEARS

The first decade of the 20th century has come to be known as The Golden Years for British Columbia. In the thrilling years just after the turn of the century, Vancouver grew faster than a field full of rain-coast mushrooms. Immigrants from all over, the greatest percentage from the British Isles, poured in, all with dreams of wealth and a better life in this resource-rich land. A much-quoted ditty from the time went "In 1910, Vancouver then will have 100,000 men!" Indeed, the population did increase from 27,000 in 1901 to more than 100,000 in 1911, with several thousand more of Oriental origin, left uncounted.

British Columbia's resource economy was booming. These were record years for the fishing, logging and mining industries, and the influx of new migrants this brought to the province created a huge escalation in the building trades. Notable buildings still standing from this era include the Carnegie Centre, Holy Rosary Cathedral, the Dominion Building, Glen Brae (Canuck Place), Gabriola Mansion, Hycroft, Aberthau, the CPR (Seabus) station, the Courthouse (now the

Advertising posters spread the word to potential immigrants.
PHILIP T. TIMMS PHOTO, CITY OF VANCOUVER ARCHIVES

ADVERTISING VANCOUVER
THE VANCOUVER INFORMATION & TOURIST ASS'N.
have placed 100 of these Posters in SEATTLE
during the A.Y.P.E. through BOND & RICKETTS

INVESTIGATE VANCOUVER
B.C. CANADA

UNLIMITED OPPORTUNITIES FOR CAPITAL

THE COMING METROPOLIS OF WESTERN AMERICA

THE ONLY TERMINAL POINT AND PORT IN CANADA ON THE PACIFIC

Art Gallery), the Sylvia Hotel, the Sun Tower, and much of the downtown infrastructure that remains today. In 1902, the first year after establishment of a Building Inspector's office, 417 building permits were issued, for structures totalling a value of $833,607. By 1910, this had soared to 2,260 permits, and the value of the buildings increased by twenty times, to $13,150,365. In 1911, the 2,800 permits issued included at least 60 for business blocks.

The speed with which the city was growing seems even more remarkable when one considers that gasoline-powered vehicles were still rare, and that much of the labour was being done with the aid of horse power alone.

It was a time of blissful ignorance. No one imagined that just around the corner lay war and hard times. So unsuspecting and giddy with success were the people of Vancouver that a 1911 promotional book titled *Modern Architecture in Vancouver B.C.* crowed optimistically, "There is not the remotest evidence of any cessation in the phenomenal increase. Don't talk of a 'Boom.' This is growth, a remarkable growth it is true. It has its origin in the awakening of the West." And the expectation was that this growth had nowhere to go but up, especially since it was believed that the eagerly anticipated Panama Canal, scheduled to open in 1914, would surely make Vancouver the largest port in the west.

It was during this period that the commercial centre of the city expanded and moved from Gastown to encompass Hastings Street from Granville to Westminster Avenue, and then crept south on both these

The Mount Pleasant Band played at the opening of the new City Market on Main Street and Terminal Avenue, August 15, 1908.

Vancouver grew faster than a field full of rain-coast mushrooms.

streets. The city was, in fact, stretching out on all sides. By 1913, Vancouver boasted 50 miles of paved streets, over a hundred miles of streetcar track, and 155 miles of interurban railway track.

Soon enough, the bubble would burst as the world slid into harsh economic times and the political situation in Europe would worsen, culminating in a catastrophic war. The optimism of the Golden Years would soon tarnish, but for a sweet, brief decade business leaders and most residents of Vancouver were convinced that the city was destined to become Canada's largest and most dynamic metropolitan centre.

Soldiers departing for the Great War, circa 1914. It was the end of an era.
STUART THOMSON PHOTO, CITY OF VANCOUVER ARCHIVES

Main Street and 17th Avenue in 1912. The neighbourhood had a small postal station in Gordon's Drugstore, but it would soon get a much grander one.

W.J. MOORE PHOTO,
CITY OF VANCOUVER ARCHIVES

CHAPTER TWO

Up She Rises

POST OFFICE EXPANSION

In the midst of these years of golden growth, Vancouver's Post Office at Granville and Pender had become inadequate for the developing city, and in 1905, the Dominion Department of Public Works contracted to erect an impressive new granite-faced Post Office building one block away on Hastings Street at the foot of Granville. By the time it opened in 1909, it was already barely adequate to the needs of the burgeoning

population, and strained under a load of 250,000 to 275,000 letters handled daily. Letters were the most rapid, reliable, and inexpensive way to stay in touch. The post was still the chief form of communication in this boom era, and the sale of postage stamps was increasing by 25 percent each year. The cost to send a local letter was just one penny, two cents for out-of-town mail.

In 1914, a convention book, published for the Federated Association of Letter Carriers, bragged that Vancouver had "by far the largest and most significant postal station in the province, a massive stone edifice looking worthy of its importance." But in spite of five daily mail deliveries in the downtown business district, and two a day to the outlying residential areas, the Central Post Office could not handle the volume single-handedly. Though this building remained the main Post Office well into the 1950s, (it is now part of the Sinclair Centre) there was a crying need for more facilities in the city. The only way to alleviate the situation was to add supplemental postal stations in the

Department of Public Works photographer George T. Wadds documented construction of Postal Station C with a series of shots (pages 16 - 20) taken between September, 1914 and the spring of 1916.
GEORGE T. WADDS PHOTOS, NATIONAL ARCHIVES OF CANADA

A decision was made to construct a substantial edifice to serve the southeast suburbs.

outlying neighbourhoods. The main office was given the name Postal Station A, and in 1914 Postal Station B was set up at 259 E. Hastings, to serve the northeast section of the city.

The decision was made to construct a substantial new edifice, to be known as Postal Station C, to serve the southeastern suburbs of Vancouver, and the adjacent city of South Vancouver. Since it was generally assumed that Mount Pleasant would become a main residential core for the city, Main Street near the edge of town at 16th Avenue was the logical location to build. It was arranged for the Department of Public Works, under the direction of Chief Architect D. Ewart, to do the job.

By this time it was 1912, the height of the economic boom not only in British Columbia but in all of Canada, a time when many post offices and other public buildings were being put up throughout the country. In such periods of extensive development, when their usual architects

Tall Tales and Local Legends

MYTH The building plans were accidentally exchanged by some clerk in Ottawa with those of the Regina Main Post Office.

REALITY Regina's Post Office was built in 1909 and is a much larger and grander building than Postal Station C ever was. Postal Station C was built in 1914, and the architect, Archibald Campbell Hope, was a Vancouver resident who would certainly have noticed if the plans had been switched.

had an excess of work, Public Works occasionally hired local design firms, and for this project they commissioned Vancouver architect Archibald Campbell Hope to draw up plans for the new postal station.

In drawing up his plans, the architect took his direction partially from one of the Department of Public Works standard styles for public buildings. A report on the building's architecture published by the Historic Sites and Monuments Board of Canada notes, " Postal Station C conforms in many respects to the 'Romanesque Retentive' type with its off-centre clock tower and steeply pitched roof. It is in its decorative vocabulary that the design breaks away from the DPW mould."

In this respect, Hope's design in some ways echoed the contemporaneous Postal Station A on Hastings Street. But he added some distinct features not found on that building, using more refined ornamental motifs and exhibiting a sense of wit in a series of carved faces, all of them anonymous except King George V, reigning monarch at the time. The elaborate ornamental scheme carved in indigenous stone demonstrates that skilled craftsmen were locally available. The ground floor walls are banded with dark-toned Haddington Island stone between layers of lighter Denman Island stone, giving a variegated look to the street level. The roof is red tile, crowned with copper ornamentation and lanterns.

A description of the design in a *Report on Public Buildings* issued by the Dominion of Canada in 1916 states, "The eclectic style of A. Campbell Hope is apparent in the façade of his asymmetrical Postal Station. He has used past orders in such a flexible manner that many of their formal characteristics are lost in his own personal vernacular."

> Hope's design echoed Postal Station A, but he added some distinct features, exhibiting a sense of wit.

19

The site chosen for the building was at the southeast corner of Main Street and 15th Avenue. A plot of land 88 feet by 73 feet was acquired from owner Samuel Elkins, a businessman and land speculator. The lot already held a residence, and the story has it that this house was moved to another of Elkins's properties a few blocks away. In July, 1914, the job of construction was awarded to contractors George E. Williamson and Thomas J. "Tom" Whiteside. Both men were prominent Mount Pleasant residents, active in church and community activities. Both had served as city councillors, Whiteside in 1909 and Williamson in 1910.

Whiteside and Williamson registered with the city for a building permit on August 26, 1914, hired Harry Burnham as crew foreman, and construction began in early September. By the following spring the job was about half complete. But the process had been slowed by the start of the Great War. Canada had entered the fray along with Britain on August 5, 1914.

Materials were in short supply, as was manpower. A story passed down in foreman Harry Burnham's family says he was instructed to hire a different crew for each floor of the building. Whether this was to spread the work around in hard times, or because men were leaving for war, we don't know. It is known that British Columbia had the highest rate of enlistment of any province, and stouthearted men who hadn't signed up were scarce. Plans had to be altered somewhat, since materials originally called for – such as Italian marble – were unavailable. But the Public Works Department soldiered on to finish the project and construction was completed in less than two years.

Even before the economic slowdown, this building was destined to be just a little too ornate for its surroundings, and perhaps a bit too big for its function as a suburban postal station, predicated as it was on the expected long-term growth of Mount Pleasant, and designed to exude the same sense of splendour as the main post office, albeit in a scaled-down version. But perhaps the building also brought a certain dignity to a neighbourhood that would suffer the humiliation of unfulfilled potential.

Contractors Williamson and Whiteside were both prominent Mount Pleasant citizens. This group portrait taken at a Presbyterian Church function shows George Williamson reclining, front row far left.

BAILEY BROS. PHOTO, CITY OF VANCOUVER ARCHIVES

Archibald Campbell Hope

LIKE ONE-THIRD OF ALL Vancouverites at the turn of the century, Archibald Campbell Hope, designer of Postal Station C, was English by birth. He was born November 28, 1870 in Bradford, Yorkshire, one of two sons and four daughters of architect Thomas Campbell Hope and his wife Mary. Archibald and his older brother Charles Edward both attended Technical School in Bradford and the two student architects articled with their father. Then both young men set out to find their fortune on the flourishing west coast of North America. The older brother, Charles, came directly to Vancouver and the younger, Archibald, made his way to San Francisco.

A few years later, Archibald had the dubious fortune of living through the great earthquake of 1906. Ironically, this was actually a lucky break for the young architect, as the construction industry prospered following the quake and resultant fire, providing him with valuable work experience. Already a member of the Royal Institute of British Architects, he now passed his exam to register with

The Hope family was rich with architects. This brother, C.E. Hope designed Alexandra House.
LANGLEY CENTENNIAL MUSEUM AND ARCHIVES

the California State Board. At the time, California was one of only two states accrediting architects, having commenced licensing in 1901.

Then in 1908, Hope made another big move, this time north to British Columbia, where a building surge was in full swing. Perhaps he was seeking the kind of success his brother had found in Canada. By then, Charles Hope had been in Vancouver for 20 years, and was well established as a real estate developer and sometime architect.

When the 38-year-old Archibald Campbell Hope arrived in Vancouver, he immediately went into practice with John S. Pearce, opening an office in the DeBeck Block at 336 West Hastings Street. Pearce & Hope were responsible for designing several schools in Vancouver, including Simon Fraser School in Mount Pleasant (which stood until 1981 when it was replaced by the present building). In 1909 the firm completed the design for the Provincial Normal School, a heritage-designated structure which has now been incorporated into the City Square shopping complex.

Within two years, Hope had moved to his own office at 603 W. Hastings. In 1912 he designed the elegant, Tudor-style Ladner Municipal Hall (which now houses the Delta Museum and Archives). Hope's

An ad for A.C. Hope's firm.
VANCOUVER CITY DIRECTORY, 1908

JOHN S. PEARCE
ARCHIBALD C. HOPE
Californian Architectural Diploma
Concrete Engineer

PEARCE & HOPE
ARCHITECTS AND ENGINEERS
Designs for Steel Frame Buildings
Reinforced Concrete Buildings

Room 3A, DeBeck Block.   336 Hastings W.   Phone 3056

Simon Fraser School, one of A.C. Hope's buildings, served Mount Pleasant students from 1909 until 1981.
W.J. MOORE PHOTO, CITY OF VANCOUVER ARCHIVES

pre-war designs are his most impressive, and his 1913 design for Postal Station C was undoubtedly his most notable work. But just as he was becoming well established, his workload, along with most of Vancouver's architects and the entire building industry, was seriously reduced by the economic downturn of 1913. After the war, he was one of the lucky ones who managed to bounce back, and continued to work steadily throughout the 1920s and '30s.

His brother Charles, meanwhile, had moved to Fort Langley where he became a prominent developer and designed several homes and commercial buildings which still stand today. (Interestingly, a row of trees planted on his farm in about 1908 or 1909 has been declared a Fort Langley municipal heritage site. The trees are California Redwoods. Could they have been brought here by Archibald when he moved north?) Another of the Hope siblings, sister Jessie, made the move from England in 1918 and also settled in Fort Langley, marrying farmer John Capel Pearse. Archibald remained in the Vancouver area, but in 1930 he was commissioned to design a Municipal Hall in Fort Langley, which continues to be a well-known community site.

Though he could not be placed in the ranks of a McClure or a Rattenbury, A.C. Hope created several prominent buildings, and fashioned a solid career in Vancouver's growing apartment sector. In the 1920s, he opened an office at 5425 West Boulevard in Kerrisdale and began an active decade, in which he planned at least ten apartment blocks, many of which are still in use. Some of the structures still in existence are: Central Hotel, 42 East Cordova Street (1921); Kirkland Metal Workshop and Stores, 6162 E. Boulevard (1926); Lilfred Lodge, 2394 Cornwall (1926); Roxborough Apartments, West 15th & Fir (1928); 1875 Yew Street (1928); and S. S. Kresge Co., 327-337 W. Hastings Street (1930).

When the Architectural Institute of British Columbia was established as a branch of the Architectural Institute of Canada, A.C. Hope became a member and remained one for his lifetime. He was also a member of the Masonic Lodge. Hope was married to Mary Helena Jane and they had one daughter, Grace Hope Stevenson, who left Vancouver to live in the United States. Archibald Campbell Hope died of heart failure on November 4, 1942, just short of his 72nd birthday, at his home at 1713 Tatlow Street, North Vancouver, leaving the lower mainland with a few more landmarks than it had when he arrived.

CHAPTER THREE

The Federal Government Era

POSTAL STATION C

In 1913, while the planning and construction of the new building progressed, a temporary location for Postal Station C was set up at 3235 Main Street on the west side of the street between 16th and 17th Avenues, just a few doors north of Hillcrest Post Office, an existing sub-station inside Gordon's Drugstore. By 1914, the temporary office had expanded to include a second location in the same block.

After a long wait for construction to finish, in Spring 1916 the new building was finally complete, and staff transferred in. For a short time, both locations were being used. It must have been a hectic few months, as staff readjusted to the larger quarters and full-service facilities.

The hammer for cancelling letters with a 'Postal Station C' postmark was proofed on May 15, 1916. Everything was in place. On June 1, 1916, Postal Station C officially opened to the public. It was a superb post office with all the best facilities.

On the ground level was a public area, with a service counter to carry out all the usual post office functions, from posting parcels to selling stamps. The interior décor was designed with practicality first, and some of the flourishes originally planned had been scaled back due to war shortages, but even so the main room was grand-looking, with shiny floors and gleaming walls, polished brasswork and an exquisite marble staircase. On the level above, the mezzanine, was an observation area with a row of small windows looking out over the public floor. An observation gallery was needed so supervisors could keep an eye on the workers on the main floor, or so the story goes. Postal Station C also provided banking services, as many post offices did in those days. In smaller communities this was often the only bank in town, but in

On June 1, 1916 the superb new Postal Station C opened to the public.

Mount Pleasant it was more of a convenience for nearby neighbours, since Main Street already boasted at least half a dozen banks.

From the outside, the building may have seemed a bit incongruous on the edge of a modest suburban neighbourhood without a lot of commercial traffic. The imposing clock tower rose high above the new post office building, its sonorous bell chiming out the hour to the empty streets below. The war was still dragging on in Europe, the economy was still in a slump, Mount Pleasant's expected growth never had materialized, and many people at the time believed the building to be unnecessarily large.

But as time went on the building's size and adaptability would prove useful. In the '20s and '30s, the volume of mail being processed there

Sorting Christmas mail at Vancouver's Main Post Office in 1913. Facilities were woefully inadequate for the city's burgeoning population.
FEDERATED ASSOCIATION OF LETTER CARRIERS CONVENTION BOOK, 1914

did increase, and the facilities were well-used. Later, the building provided space enough for the Dominion Department of Agriculture to establish a seed laboratory, and later still the RCMP set up a temporary forensic laboratory there.

In the 1940s, when the Post Office and the Department of Agriculture shared the facility, the building was actually overcrowded. After World War II, the postal system underwent major alterations, and at that time the operations of Postal Station C were moved to another location.

Albert Lawrence was one of the letter carriers at Postal Station C in the late '40s and early '50s. "During the time I worked there," he says, "the Post Office was on the main floor and the Department of Agriculture had the second floor. It was an important office and carried out quite a lot of government business besides the post office. There were about six or seven clerks working in the public office, and as many as 40 or more letter carriers working out of that station."

"The building was badly overcrowded when I was there. You could hardly move, there were so many people working there. As the area built

Cancellation hammer for Postal Station C was proofed in May, 1916. The Carrier in Charge for Station C was F. Buckley, below.

FEDERATED ASSOCIATION OF LETTER CARRIERS CONVENTION BOOK, 1914

Tall Tales and Local Legends

MYTH The volume of mail was so low that in 1922 the Post Office moved out and the Dominion Department of Agriculture moved in.

REALITY Wrong on both counts. While the building was a little roomy for its original function, the Post Office was the sole occupant until the Department of Agriculture took over the second floor – in 1937. The two offices shared the location until 1950, when the Post Office finally vacated – due to lack of space.

up, there were more and more people working there until we had to work out of the basement. The letter carriers would go out in the morning, and then come back to the building at noon, to do our office work, then go out again in the afternoon. We spent a lot of our time travelling. We travelled by streetcar in those days."

He recalls that they were particularly busy during the holiday season. "Sometimes at Christmas time we worked late into the night, and after work we'd go over to Bert's Cafeteria, across from the streetcar barns at 13th & Main, because it was open late into the night. It was a favourite place for the streetcar drivers. They would be coming and going at all hours."

Albert says the Post Office began moving out in 1949. "The public office, which was in the front part of the building, moved down to Broadway, between Main and Quebec Street, and then later it moved again, up to 10th & Quebec. After that, just the letter carriers worked in the building until 1952." This made the ground floor available to the Department of Agriculture. A small mail-sorting operation stayed on in the basement, serving as a pick-up and drop-off point for the remaining letter carriers.

Along with overcrowded conditions, Albert says another reason for discontinuing the post office there was that they were serving a very large area, including most of Southeast Vancouver, from Cambie over to Joyce and Kingsway. When the last of the letter carriers were assigned to several other postal stations, the Postal Station C building became the exclusive domain of the Department of Agriculture.

Letter carriers went out in the morning, came back for lunch, then went out again. They travelled by streetcar.

The Caretakers

MANY LIVES HAVE TOUCHED this building, but none have had a more close-up view of the old dowager than the men who looked after her throughout the years. For 47 years of Heritage Hall's history, caretakers stoked the furnace, shooed away the pigeons, repaired the ravages of time, wound the clock, and made their homes in the attic suite.

When Postal Station C opened its doors in 1916, the building was under the care of Robert Forgie, a 49-year-old Scotsman. He and his wife Mary had come to Canada in 1908, with their son and four daughters. For the first few years, he worked for B.C. Electric, and then was offered the job of looking after the new neighbourhood postal station. Robert and Mary moved in and stayed for an 11-year tenure. They were a close family, and the now grownup children often stopped by. Robert Jr. lived just around the corner. One daughter, Ann Heslip, was newly married and, at 18, expecting her first child. When it was time for the baby to arrive, she came to her mother for midwifery. And so it was that in November, 1916, Mary Heslip (Mary 'Pat' Vincent) was born in the top-floor suite, Postal Station C's very own "special delivery."

The Forgies lived in the building until 1927, and had no intention of leaving, until Archibald Chisholm, Robert's friend and a fellow caretaker at the Main Post Office downtown, called on him with a proposition. Archie, it seems, wasn't getting any younger. Already over the age of 80, he'd been caretaking the imposing Postal Station A since it opened in 1909, and the task was becoming a bit overwhelming for the old chap. He wanted to trade positions with his younger buddy, and Forgie agreed willingly, since it meant a promotion for him. But the plan, which seemed like a good idea, turned out badly for both men. For Robert Forgie, the switch was tragic. Less than a year after moving into the larger building, he fell into the elevator shaft and was taken to St. Paul's hospital with major injuries. He died three days later on April 30, 1928.

Archie Chisholm fared better than his friend, but perhaps he hadn't thought the move through sufficiently. For one thing, his wife Mary (who was

After many years caretaking the Main Post Office, Archie Chisholm moved to Postal Station C at age 80.

Tall Tales and Local Legends

MYTH One of the caretakers brewed beer in the building, another one bred dogs upstairs, and one caretaker's wife was a clairvoyant.

REALITY We haven't been able to verify any of these stories – though the remnants of something resembling a still were found when the building was renovated.

more than 20 years younger than Archie) was furious about leaving their beautiful harbour-view apartment and moving down into the more humble quarters on Main Street. But that wasn't the worst of it. Though Chisholm was still a robust man who stood tall and upright, his 80-year-old legs just couldn't manage the difficult climb up the steep stairs to the clock tower. In 1930, after only three years, they retired, and went to live with their daughter's family. His grandchildren remember him as a kindly, bearded fellow who took them out for walks around their Kerrisdale neighbourhood.

Next to take over the care of the Post Office was Frank Connolly. A small, sturdy man, Connolly had come to Canada from Ireland as a sailor, arriving in Vancouver in about 1927, when he was in his early 40s. Here he met Emily Gillespie, a young widow ten years his junior, they were married, and he settled down in Vancouver for good. Of all the caretakers, Connolly held the job the longest time, staying in the building for 19 years. When he began, in 1930,

the entire building was occupied by the Postal Department, but seven years later the Dominion Agriculture Department began their tenancy of the second floor, while postal services remained on the main floor. In 1949, the public portion of the post office moved out, and in the same year Connolly retired. But Frank and Emily continued to think of Mount Pleasant as home, for they moved into a house just a few blocks away, and remained there the rest of their lives.

When Connolly retired, his assistant, W. Charles Freeman, who was already living next door, moved the family – his wife, two children, the inlaws, and the dog – up to the "penthouse" and took over as live-in caretaker. By that time, the

The caretaker's third floor bathroom contained some fine tile work and a comfortable bathtub.

CANADIAN INVENTORY OF HISTORIC BUILDINGS PHOTO

only postal function still operating out of the building was mail distribution to letter carriers, and within a few years, this too would be phased out. Meanwhile, the Agriculture Department gradually took over more and more of the building's area.

Freeman was a veteran of both World Wars, and was plagued by a back injury from his first stint in the service. But he was a diligent worker, and he had two strong sons to share some of the workload. Freeman was also a resourceful handyman who put a lot of creative energy into making the post office building a real home for his family. Both of his sons have fond memories of their days there, which they speak about in a separate section of this book. The Freemans lived in the building until 1954, when the family moved to Salt Spring Island.

Then the final live-in caretaker, Frederick J. Baker, moved in and remained there until 1963. Even after moving out, he continued to come and wind the clock each week. Baker looked after the building from the time the Agriculture Department took over the entire premises until the time the RCMP moved out. Baker was English by birth. He was 13 when his family emigrated to Canada. Conscientious and hardworking by nature, he was employed for many years by the 4X Bakery at 10th and Ash. He and his wife Ruth raised their family in Mount Pleasant, in a home on Howard Street and 13th Avenue. After the bakery closed, Baker was offered the live-in position at the federal building just two blocks away, and it gave the 56-year-old the opportunity to keep working. Baker's son Frank remembers visiting his folks there and tossing a football around with his sister's kids in one large area inside the building.

There was a certain symmetry in Baker being the final live-in caretaker. As a young man, he had worked with the construction crew that built the place, hauling gravel for the foundation in a horse-drawn truck.

Anne Heslip, daughter of caretaker Robert Forgie, with her daughter Mary who was born in the building. Taken on the third floor roof deck.

Tall Tales and Local Legends

MYTH The old meat freezers on the second floor were renovated to become offices. Portions of the building were used to store the carcasses of diseased animals.

REALITY There were never any meat freezers in the building. No animal products, diseased or otherwise, were ever stored in the building.

DOMINION DEPARTMENT OF AGRICULTURE

The Department of Agriculture had been using portions of the building since May, 1937, when the department moved a section of their offices from Granville and Pender to Postal Station C, occupying the second floor of the building, while the post office retained the ground floor. There was to be a new seed testing laboratory created, the first one in British Columbia. Even though the federal government had enacted the Seeds Act back in 1904, up until this time B.C. had sent samples to labs on the prairies for testing.

The Seeds Act set out the standards that commercial seed had to meet. Before seed product could go on the market, it had to be tested and

Analysts Connie Plommer and Marie Mason planting cereals and peas to test germination percentages.
HELEN SINCLAIR COLLECTION

Binder twine awaiting
quality control.
HELEN SINCLAIR COLLECTION

found to meet stringent government standards. Several tests were done to each batch of seeds. Seed was checked for weed seed contamination, for quality and percentage of germination, and had to meet a certain level of purity.

Estelle Lavine worked for the Seed Branch in the 1960s, and though the lab was set up well before her time there, she knows the story well. "When the lab opened in 1937," she explains in a voice that still holds more than a trace of an English accent, "they brought in an analyst from the Winnipeg office and he and another chap started the lab." The second floor was renovated to accommodate facilities consisting of offices, a Seed Germination Room and a Purity Room. "The lab was built in an area where they used to store coal," Estelle relates. The area where the Germination Room was to be built was so dark and dingy that staff jokingly referred to it as the Black Hole of Calcutta.

When the Plant Products division was in full swing, it employed around ten analysts, a district analyst, and support staff. Estelle was the assistant to the District Analyst. "The District Analyst produced a lot of literature, based on the tests conducted in the lab," she explains. "The lab

The Seed Branch displayed
their work at agricultural
fairs throughout the
Lower Mainland.
HELEN SINCLAIR COLLECTION

33

was an ivory tower; it had no direct contact with the commercial seed trade. Only the District Analyst and one or two others had contact with the trade. If there was a problem, it was conveyed to the manufacturers through the administration."

As well as doing analysis under the Seeds Act, the department was also involved in administering the Fertilizer Act, the Pesticide Act, and the Binder Twine Act.

The mention of the Binder Twine Act brings a smile to Estelle's face. It seems that even back then, technology didn't always work as it was meant to, and some improvisation was necessary. She recalls, "When the binder twine came in, random samples had to be measured to see if it met the required length, as labelled. There was a machine to measure the length. But the machine didn't always work accurately. In the lab area, there were green floor tiles, one-foot square. I have this mental picture of us down on our knees, measuring out the binder twine against the floor tiles."

In the years that Estelle worked there, the entire building was occupied by divisions of the Dominion Department of Agriculture.

Analysts Connie Plommer, Marie Mason, and Helen Sinclair in the Germination Room.

"Plant Products, which was the seed lab, was upstairs," she says. "Downstairs was Livestock, Poultry, and Health of Animals, which were three separate units of Agriculture. The seed lab was the only lab doing testing there; downstairs was just offices."

The ground floor filled up with Department of Agriculture administrative offices for the Livestock and Health of Animals branches.

G.M. Stewart, District Supervisor of Plant Products Division, 1937-1948, seated in his second floor office.
HELEN SINCLAIR COLLECTION

The office looked after some personnel and payroll records, but the main activity was to generate inspection reports to Ottawa on the conditions of livestock on farms, and of meat in processing facilities. Certified vets, with the assistance of lay inspectors, would routinely check livestock quarters for infectious illnesses, while other vets examined slaughterhouses for such health risks as bacterial contamination.

Dr. H.K. Chen was one of the veterinarians who inspected abattoirs. He started working in the Health of Animals branch in 1954. Dr. Chen remembers that Vancouver had six large slaughterhouses, which were inspected regularly. The samples were sent to an outside lab and the results reported back to District Veterinary Inspector Frederick W.B. Smith at the Main Street office. No animal testing was done in the building, he says. The Livestock and Health of Animals units used the building strictly for administrative functions.

The total staff in the building during the Agriculture years was about 40 or 50 people, as Estelle Lavine recalls. She says, "We had a staff of probably 20 to 25 in Plant Products, and another 20 to 25 worked in the downstairs offices."

In the intervening years, the number of government seed labs has shrunk considerably, to be supplanted by commercial testing labs. In fact, when the Vancouver lab closed, Estelle and several other staff

members got together and established a commercial lab themselves. Nowadays, only Ottawa and Saskatoon have government-run labs.

Estelle's memories of her time in the building on Main Street are all pleasant. "The building at that time had so much atmosphere, with the marble stairs. There was a kind of a rooftop deck, and everybody would sunbathe there at noontime. It was a wonderful place. It holds many happy memories for me."

She remembers many amusing anecdotes from those days, but one of the most vivid is of their last day in the building, sometime in 1963, before the department moved out to new quarters in the Customs Building at Pender and Burrard.

"I remember the last day that we were there, we had all of us always wanted to go up into the bell tower, but we were never allowed to. So, on that day, I don't know who gave consent, but someone did, and all of us trooped up just as the hour struck and the bell chimed….or at least in my memory it did! It was very emotional. Our last memory of the building, all of us going up one after the other. It's just a wonderful building, and it really was a privilege to work there."

A sunny Monday morning in the spotless office of the Department of Agriculture.
HELEN SINCLAIR COLLECTION

Estelle Lavine at her desk at the Seed Branch.
HELEN SINCLAIR COLLECTION

A Unique Childhood

LYLE AND BARRY FREEMAN HAVE a unique perspective on Heritage Hall. As the sons of caretakers Charles and Elizabeth Freeman, the two spent their formative years living there. When Barry was four and Lyle was two, their father was hired as assistant to then-caretaker Frank Connolly, and for five years the Freeman family lived in the tiny cottage next door. Then, in 1949, Connolly retired and the Freemans moved up in the world – up to the top floor of Postal Station C, that is.

The brothers, both of them now over the age of 60, have vivid memories of the building, most of them pleasant and a few not so pleasant. But there's no doubt, the family did a lot of living in their post office penthouse.

Even though Barry recollects that, "We were poor as church mice," and that there was always lots of hard work for the boys to do, he admits he does retain a certain affection for the place.

Lyle pictures the scene in a somewhat brighter light, "It was kind of neat living there. It was the biggest building around that area, and we had the best view from our bedroom. There was the Post Office on the first floor, and the Department of Agriculture on the second floor, and our suite was on the top floor. The two "towers" on the building were bedrooms. One was for the adults and the other one was the kids' bedroom."

"Outside the back door of the suite," he recalls,

Charles Freeman in a snapshot taken on the building roof deck by amateur photographer Barry.

"there was a kind of a wood-floored veranda. Part of it was a deck, and another area sort of like a courtyard a few steps down, and that's where my mother hung the clothesline."

"We did everything on that balcony," Barry says, "It was like a back yard, only better, cause it was protected. That's where I'd fire my BB gun. We had a garden up there, in pots. We grew carrots, onions, and radishes."

Lyle laughs, "We'd invite the neighbourhood kids up there to play and we'd fill balloons with water and drop them down onto Watson St. – we never threw them at people or anything – in those days we did it innocently."

Lyle and Barry may have been innocent kids, but they were a little on the mischievous side.

"After business hours were finished," Lyle remembers, "my brother and I had free rein of that building. We never did any damage, but in the evenings we'd go in all the offices, sit at the desks. I can remember the old telephones they had, where

you'd pick it up and the operator would ask you what number you wanted. We'd play with those phones, they were just toys to us. The Department of Agriculture had these little fine scales for weighing seeds, and we'd play with them too. We'd weigh paper clips on them."

In those days, kids were allowed a great deal of independence. The neighbourhood still had pockets of bush, where they'd spend many an afternoon playing Hide and Seek or Cowboys and Indians. When they'd exhausted all the games, the boys used to ride the streetcars and trolley buses to go visit their grandparents over at 38th and Fraser Street, or to go to Kivan Boys' Club where Barry liked to go to and develop the photographs he'd taken.

Meanwhile, back at home, there was always lots going on, and plenty of chores to be done.

"When we lived there," says Lyle, "letter carriers worked out of there. I can remember half a dozen or more of them coming in in the morning to get their bags, then they'd come back at noon and sit out behind the building to eat lunch, and they'd talk to my brother and me, and then go out on their afternoon route."

The Freeman brothers on the roof deck. Lyle holds their dog Fifi, and Barry holds little cousin Linda.

They had an ice box, and Barry can still picture the ice man cursing as he carried the week's supply of ice on a leather pad on his back, straining to get up the three flights of stairs.

In the rear of the building was a coal chute. Lyle describes the coal delivery, "An old truck would arrive with coal in burlap sacks, and the guys would open the sacks and dump the coal down the chute into a big bin."

But the brothers couldn't just stand back and watch the activities. They were always expected to do their fair share, and one of their jobs was to get that coal up from the basement to the top floor. "Our coal for the stove had to come up from the basement," Barry says. "It was dumped into the coal bin from Watson Street and then we hauled it up the stairs a bucket at a time. My father was a disabled war vet, so thankfully even at an early age I was strong enough to help him do these things."

Their father in fact was a veteran of both World Wars. At 15, he joined the army and came back with a back injury. Then in the Second World

War, he served in the Veteran's Guard. But his old injury always plagued him, especially in his later years. As Barry puts it, "You could see the holes in him!"

Their father wasn't physically strong, but he was both a family man and a handyman, and any spare time he had usually went into improving their living quarters. His hobby was woodworking, and he had a workshop with a lathe and table saws, up in a utility area they called the 'upstairs basement.' He built the boys a bedroom in one of the towers, and later when their mother's parents moved in with them, he fixed up another room for the boys just under the clock tower. According to Lyle, the chiming of the bell above their heads never woke them up. But every Saturday morning they had to get up anyway, to help their dad wind the clock mechanism.

One Christmas, the brothers got a train set, and "from then on," Lyle reports, "we just kept adding to it. We got switches, and we built lakes and rivers and trees and mountains and we got more and more tables until it filled up half the upstairs basement. We spent hours and hours in there, and all the neighbourhood kids would come up and play with this electric train set. It was the O gauge type, with the three-rail tracks. We had all kinds of switches. Our dad helped build it, but we played with it, not him."

In 1954, when Barry was 14 and Lyle was 12, the family moved out of the city to a new home on Salt Spring Island. Their father got a job in the federal building in Victoria, and eventually, to lessen his commute, they moved there.

Today, Lyle and Barry are both retired, but there's still a touch of the playful boy in each of the brothers – Barry is still into model railroading, and Lyle is a collector of old toys. Once, he revisited his childhood home when an antique toy show was held there.

"We did everything on that balcony." Elizabeth Freeman and Fifi pose near the dartboard. BARRY FREEMAN PHOTO

ROYAL CANADIAN MOUNTED POLICE

The dust from the Department of Agriculture's move hardly had time to settle before the next tenant started moving in. RCMP headquarters in Ottawa had decided that a new forensic laboratory should be established in Vancouver for the British Columbia and Yukon region. Four staff would be relocated here, three from the Regina Laboratory and one from Ottawa.

The lab was offered a choice of three federally owned sites, but one was unsuitable and another wasn't ready immediately, so the old Post Office building was picked as a temporary site until the other location was available, although it was larger than the small staff really needed.

Don N. Brown, who transferred from Ottawa, recalls, "The three members from Regina arrived in June of 1963 and set up shop. They included a staff sergeant who was a chemist, a corporal with a specialty in firearms and allied identifications, and a civilian member in charge of serology. I arrived in July, to be sergeant in charge of the documents section. A fifth member joined us from Regina in September, a corporal who would manage the hair and fibre section."

As it turned out, the location worked out well, and the staff became quite fond of it. "We were extremely busy from the day we walked into the old building," Don says. "It wasn't unusual to 'burn the midnight candle' in preparing cases for court on an urgent basis, or coming down to the lab in the wee hours of the night to pick up exhibits for an early flight out of town, and the creaking, groaning and rattling noises to be heard in that building in the late hours made us certain that they were being made by the 'ghosts' of long ago postal employees, dragging sacks of mail across the floors, or incessantly stamping envelopes...quite scary at 3 a.m."

"The creaking, groaning and rattling noises heard in the late hours made us certain they were being made by the 'ghosts' of long ago postal employees, dragging sacks of mail across the floors..."

Tall Tales and Local Legends

MYTH The RCMP used the building for wire-tapping surveillance operations in the 1960s.

REALITY If there's any truth to this one, the RCMP still aren't telling! They say, "It never happened."

The lab remained in the building until the summer of 1965 when it moved into a more permanent home at 33rd and Fraser, but Don points out that by that time they had become accustomed to the noises of the place and didn't really want to leave it.

"Nearly 40 years have now passed," he says, "since a small contingent of scientists opened the first RCMP forensic laboratory in British Columbia, and every time I drive down Main Street and pass the old building, pangs of nostalgia engulf me."

After the lab left the building, other RCMP units took up residence there. Vancouver's local detachment, known as the Vancouver Town Station, occupied the ground floor and the Crime Index Section took over the second floor.

The Vancouver Town Station moved from the Fairmont office at Heather and 33rd Avenue when that office needed more space for a newly created training facility. Bob Owens, who was in the detachment at the time, can still picture the layout of the Main Street office, "Right inside the main front door was our public counter for people coming in with inquiries. Then there was the NCO's office in the northwest corner by the windows, and the office next to that was the Court Records man,

For slow times in the 24-hour-a-day schedule, table tennis was available in the basement.
CANADIAN INVENTORY OF HISTORIC BUILDINGS PHOTO

At one point the Crime Index Section was so busy they needed six telex machines.

CANADIAN INVENTORY OF HISTORIC BUILDINGS PHOTO

who looked after the prisoners. Just to the right of the main door there was a little room that we used for a change room, and next to that was our coffee room."

The main responsibilities of the detachment were to look after prisoners, making sure they appeared when and where they were scheduled. Bob recounts, "Vancouver Town Station would escort prisoners out to all the prisons. We'd go to the airport and meet prisoners being brought in on airplanes from all over B.C."

Ten to 15 constables worked in the Town Station at a time, most of them working a six-month or one-year tour of duty before being sent to assignments in other parts of the province. "It was a very mobile place," recalls Bruce Lindsay, who worked in the Vancouver Town Station in 1970. "We went in and got our duties for the day and then left. We did a lot of things like warrant, summons and subpoena duty in Vancouver, and escorting prisoners. Picking them up at the airport, delivering them to the various institutions, such as the B.C. Penitentiary, Oakalla, and Riverview. There was a lot of road work, as I remember."

"They put the more junior people in there, to sort of season us a bit. We learned the city, and how to deal with prisoners. We also went down to the old courthouse downtown, where we were given assize court duties or supreme court duties. We'd take our prisoners up to the court and sit with them in court. Sometimes you'd work there two or three days at a time. We were always on the move."

The main responsibilities of the detachment were to look after prisoners, making sure they appeared when and where they were scheduled.

Meanwhile, another RCMP agency occupied the second floor of the building. The Crime Index Section (CIS) was a completely different kind of office, and the two sections had very little contact with each other.

The CIS was a criminal records section which kept reports and running files on known criminals, to keep track of their movements and activities. The agency did not usually deal directly with the public. Instead, it worked closely with RCMP investigators, acting as a central database for detachments throughout the province. Computers weren't in common use back then, so the Crime Index Section was the main information repository for the whole province.

Reg Chase, who was with the CIS at the time, explains, "Each detachment around B.C. maintained its own criminal profiles for individuals within their detachment area, but during the '60s and '70s criminals were becoming increasingly mobile. So our section was designed to set up profiles on active criminals, ones that were worth watching, throughout the whole of B.C. And we were also the contact for any inquiries from outside the province."

Reg started in the CIS as a shift worker, working on the phones and the telex, later a shift supervisor, then a unit supervisor who was eventually put in charge of the section. He was with the section the entire ten-year period that their offices were in the building.

The RCMP detachment made creative use of the old post office vault, ammunition was stored in it.

CANADIAN INVENTORY OF HISTORIC BUILDINGS PHOTO

He remembers it as a place where the staff worked hard, and had a lot of fun. "I used to enjoy it. It was one of the most fun places that I was ever stationed. We weren't under the direct thumb of headquarters, and people who came there came for a purpose, to get their job done. We weren't bothered by any internal politics. We just went about our business, and did our work well. We were a 24-hour-a-day, seven-day-a-week operation. We even had a ping-pong table set up for breaks."

42

"That building had a lot of character to it. When we'd get new personnel in, we'd give them a tour around the premises and we always made sure that we took them up into the belfry just as the clock was about to strike 11."

"There wasn't any air conditioning….you'd just open up the windows, and get enough of a cross draft that you'd have to watch that your papers weren't flying out the window." He chuckles, "And we had pigeons that used to nest in the windows – and we'd feed the suckers, so that didn't help either. We'd bring in rye seed, and put water out for the little ones. It was a bit of wildlife."

Several other small RCMP sections operated in the building as well. Reg recalls, "For about a year and a half we had our radio section (Telecoms) there. That was strictly mobile radio contact. And telex. We got so busy at one point we had six telex machines going. The force tailor was in that little mezzanine section, and Quartermaster Stores were on the ground floor. They stored various items there – car tires and decals, clothing, seasonal and sundry items – and the ammunition was stored in the vault."

The Crime Index Section was the last RCMP agency to occupy the premises. Vancouver Town Station moved out in 1972, but Crime Index Section stayed on until 1976. When it left, the old building sat empty and deteriorating, but still as imposing as ever. Too imposing, many have said; too ostentatious. But it may have been this excessive grandeur that saved its life and gave it one more incarnation, as Heritage Hall.

There was no air conditioning. You'd just open up the windows and watch that your papers didn't fly out.

CHAPTER FOUR

Saving the Building

THE IDEA

It hadn't taken long for some sharp-eyed community organizations to take note of the deserted federal government building on the corner of 15th and Main. Charles Christopherson, who was active in the Brewery Creek Historical Society and the Mount Pleasant Citizen's Planning Committee maintains that local community groups were interested in using the building almost as soon as the RCMP moved out in 1976.

Charles Keast was involved with the Satellite Video Exchange Society (now Video In) and was also a board member of the Greater Vancouver Information and Referral Service (now Information Services Vancouver). It was Charles's ideas and organizational skills which led to what eventually became the successful bid for the building. In the late '70s, he pulled together a few friends and acquaintances from various non-profit agencies and pitched them an idea. What if they could gain access to the building for use as shared office space and a community communications facility? What if they could fix up and renovate the grande old dame and at the same time make her useful again? Who would they have to convince that the idea had merit? Who would be involved? How would they raise the necessary money?

Gil Evans was the executive director of the Greater Vancouver Information and Referral Service. He remembers, "Charlie found out the building was available and he set out to put together a group of organizations to try to acquire the building. That fell through, but the idea didn't leave his head."

The building had been declared a heritage structure by the federal government in 1976 and had been included on the City of Vancouver's first Heritage List in 1974. Despite, (or perhaps because of) this heritage designation, the federal government had left the building unused for

Could they fix up and renovate the grande old dame and make her useful again?

several years. During that time the building was offered to other federal departments and also to the Province and the City. All offers were declined. The building was vacant and suffering vandalism and was beginning to be considered a liability. By 1980, Public Works Canada was looking at ways to divest itself of the building.

Andria Spindell, executive director of the Social Planning and Review Council (SPARC) of B.C., led the next wave of community interest in the building. Building on Keast's original ideas, Spindell and

The old building sat empty and deteriorating from 1976 until early 1981.

45

several other agencies, now calling themselves the Main Source project, got serious about getting access to the building in late 1980.

Ironically, the interested groups were not primarily motivated by the architectural or historical merits of the building. Their needs were first and foremost financial. Roy Crowe, who worked with Vancouver Volunteer Centre, one of the non-profits which ultimately occupied the building, remembers two things which motivated his agency's involvement: a spike in the Vancouver real estate market and being urged to leave the offices they occupied in the United Way building. Says Roy, "It was just impossible to take any commercial lease at that time. They were five times what we were paying at the United Way, and we were a pretty hard-up little organization."

While saving money might not seem the most noble reason to save an outstanding heritage building, money was not a trivial matter to struggling non-profit community agencies. The amount of energy expended to stablilize the rental costs of a few non-profit groups would, in the end, be staggering.

Peeling paint and missing floor tiles in the south west corner of the second floor.

THE CAST OF CHARACTERS

Apart from two exceptions, the non-profit groups who started the initiative did not end up being the ones who ultimately moved into the building. In the beginning there was the Satellite Video Exchange Society, the Social Planning and Review Council (SPARC) of B.C., the B.C. Association of Social Workers, the Vancouver Volunteer Centre and Voluntary Action Resource Centre, and the Greater Vancouver Information and Referral Service. Along the way the cast changed to include the Vancouver Volunteer Centre, Information Services Vancouver, Association of Neighbourhood Houses, Junior League of Greater Vancouver, Avenue of the Arts (who were eventually asked to leave the group), and later the Writers' Union of Canada and the Vancouver Little Theatre. Of course, there were many talented non-affiliated citizens who were interested in helping out with a worthwhile endeavour and community groups like the Mount Pleasant Local Area Planning Committee were also involved.

The roof was in dire need of repair.

After shuffling the membership deck more that a couple of times, the group, which would officially become the Main Source Management Society on March 29, 1982 got busy on their grand vision of what the building could become.

GETTING THE GOVERNMENT ON-SIDE

Since the building had been declared a significant heritage structure by both the City of Vancouver and the federal government in the mid-'70s, it was not in any real danger of falling prey to the wrecking ball. Public Works Canada had a building assessment done in 1980-81 which said the structure would require $1.2 million in repairs to bring it up to standard.

By January 1981, the federal government was considering disposing of the property by public tender. The loose collection of non-profit

ARCHITECTURE

Postal Station 'C' is a nearly square two-storey block with projecting pavilions, tower and high-hipped roof covered in slate. The ground floor is banded Haddington Island stone over a plinth of selected Denman Island stone; the floor above is buff Roman brick with stone trim. The building is richly ornamented with pilasters with vaguely Corinthian capitals, half of which incorporate sculpted faces; swags and festoons; dentillated cornice and string course; and various other mouldings all carved in stone. The roof is equally ornamental, with scalloped patterns in the slate, and large crockets marking the transition from pyramidal roofs to domes and pinnacles...

From Public Works Canada Prospectus,
Appendix B, year not known.

COUPLED PILASTERS

SCULPTURED COLUMNS

MECHANICAL CHIMING CLOCK WITH FOUR FACES

WROUGHT IRON CRESTING

CARVED FACE OF KING GEORGE V

COPPER ROOF

RED TILE WITH COPPER ORNAMENTATION

CHATEAU-STYLE WOOD FRAME ROOF WITH SLATE COVERING

49

CARVED STONE FESTOONS AND GARLANDS

ROUGH TEXTURED BANDS OF DENMAN ISLAND STONE

SMOOTH BANDS OF HADDINGTON ISLAND STONE

DOUGLAS KENNEDY PHOTOS
GERRY APUADA ILLUSTRATION

"I am often asked about the architectural style of the building. I say it is French Chateau with clock tower an important feature, seen through British eyes, with Federal Ottawa overlay of 1913. A French chateau in a modern reinforced concrete frame with an asbestos tile roof. Unconventional indeed."

Wolfgang Gerson, from his speech on the day Heritage Hall opened to public use, November 20, 1983

agencies had already approached the City and the Province to ask them to help acquire the property and restore it for use by their social, community and cultural organizations. The City liked the idea and even funded a feasibility study. Public Works delayed its tender to allow the City time to put together a proposal. At this point, the City was unable to put in a bid because the agencies were not yet unanimous in their intentions for the building and because of the over $1 million in renovation costs.

The City liked the idea and even funded a feasibility study.

So the Public Works tender went public in September 1981, with a deadline of October 28. When Main Source got wind of the tender, they realized that this could be their last chance to give the building the kind of future they had envisioned. Main Source offered to lease the property from Public Works for a term of 51 years for a rental of $1 per year but they also secured support from Max Beck, Director of Social Planning for the City of Vancouver, who presented their latest proposal to an October 20, 1981 City Council meeting. Assuming they could secure a lease for the building, Main Source proposed a funding formula that asked each of three levels of government and the private sector to contribute 25 percent of restoration costs. A letter dated October 27, 1981 from Mayor Mike Harcourt to Public Works Canada asked for an opportunity to discuss alternate proposals "in the event Public Works Canada is not able to agree to a lease with the Main Source." This was one day before the tender's closing date – the proverbial eleventh hour!

Gil Evans was the executive director of the Greater Vancouver Information and Referral Service. He recalls that Dr. Ernest Wong, a Vancouver psychiatrist, was the highest bidder in the tender. "He planned to make his home and office on the top floors and run an antique business on the main floor." Wong's bid was for $387,000 and Public Works was seriously considering accepting it. Since there were cash offers for the building, Public Works was unable to agree to a non-monetary lease with Main Source. But the federal agency agreed the building should remain in the public domain if possible, and gave the City of Vancouver until December 17 to waive their right to first refusal.

They also discussed an alternate proposal with the City's Social

Planning Department which recommended the City of Vancouver offer $62,500 (half the assessed land value) to purchase the building. Public Works set three conditions to the pending sale: the property would only be used for non-commercial public purposes; the heritage aspect of the building would be respected; and if those conditions were not met, or if the City of Vancouver made any attempt to dispose of the building, the federal government reserved the right to reacquire the property.

City Council subsequently approved the purchase of the building for the recommended $62,500 and agreed to lease it to the Main Source agencies to restore and run. City Council recommended future councils approve Capital Grants of up to $300,000. Restoration costs were estimated to be between $500,000 and $1.2 million. For its part, Main Source had to secure the rest of the funding from wherever it could. It was a huge task, one that occupied Main Source for over three years.

The City's chief social planner, Max Beck, and his staff, especially Tony Mears, provided support and advice along the way to securing the building. Various politicians, including Senator Jack Austen, Margaret Mitchell, M.P., Grace McCarthy, M.L.A., Mayor Mike Harcourt and city councillor Harry Rankin all supported the project.

Nancy McKenzie lived in the neighbourhood and at the time chaired the Mount Pleasant Local Area Planning Committee. She points out that it was remarkable how different levels of government worked together with the non-profits so the societies could operate in a self-sufficient manner. "There was just so much good will about the whole idea, a perfect marriage of restoring a significant heritage building, societies able to operate out of that building, and the public being able to use and enjoy it," says Nancy. "There were no down sides as far as I could tell."

—Vancouver Public Library photo

The Main Street building, dating from 1915, has been empty for five years.

51

New group eyes stately building

■ Architectural historian Harold Kalman calls it "Vancouver's best example of beaux arts classicism." But the building began prosaically in 1915 as Postal Station C.

"It was intended to dominate its low neighbors," Kalman wrote, "for the top storey originally had no use." And a recent Public Works report on the building comments that the design is "quite sophisticated ... the execution of its elaborate ornamental scheme in local stone shows that a body of skilled craftsmen was available to the builders."

The building, at Main and East 15th in Vancouver, has had a number of different tenants since it opened, but has been vacant for five years. Now a local group wants to restore it to public use. More on that in a moment.

The stone and brick building was designed by architect **Archibald Campbell Hope** after he moved here from San Francisco. Hope also designed the Central Hotel on East Cordova.

It's said Hope was inspired by the clock on England's parliament buildings, and that's why there is a mechanical clock on the tallest tower. It still works.

In 1922, new tenants replaced the post office and the structure became the Dominion Agriculture Building. That's what the sign over the Main Street door says to this day, even though the aggies moved out in 1962.

The building was vacant for three years, and then was occupied by the RCMP from 1965 to 1976. During their tenancy, it was designated as a heritage building, included in the first list of buildings to be identified by the city as having historical importance.

Now a proposal has been made to bring life back to the building. It's called The Main Source. It consists of a group of voluntary, non-profit organizations providing community services to the province and the city.

So far, the list includes SPARC (Social Planning and Review Council of B.C.), the B.C. Association of Social Workers, the Vancouver Volunteer Centre, the Voluntary Action Resource Centre, the Greater Vancouver Information and Referral Service.

They want to pool resources under one roof, and they want a 51-year lease from the federal government.

The organizers plan "to restore the building according to the heritage guidelines making it a vital

Chuck Davis

and active centre in the Mount Pleasant Community." They'll undertake repairs and renovations to the building, if they get it.

■ Incidentally, reading about the old building's construction, I came across this: "The exceptional ornamental carving was carried out in Haddington Island stone. This stone was also used on the Hotel Vancouver and on the courthouse."

That "Haddington Island stone" reference has popped up several times in my research into various Vancouver buildings. It's time, I thought, to find out more about this stone.

First, you'll want to know that Haddington Island itself is a tiny dot of land off the east coast of Vancouver Island near Alert Bay.

The stone, according to a back issue of the Victoria Naturalist, is an ancient lava. "At the Haddington Island quarry," says the magazine, "we see the result of forces pressing from the northeast, causing the lava and the cretaceous sediments to be compressed into close folds with some over-thrusting. The color of the rock varies from light yellow to a greyish tone. It is ... easily shaped, and its chiseled form has a quality of beauty as well as durability.

"Some years ago, **Archdeacon Robert Connell** ground a flake of it so thin that it was fairly transparent under a microscope using reflected light."

■ I didn't have the space in last Sunday's column (about the anniversary of the opening of the main branch of the Vancouver Public Library) to include a recollection of a poignant event. It so happens that in 1924 a young man named **Edgar Robinson** was hired as librarian. He ran the system for 33 years, struggling constantly to persuade council to increase the library's book budget, and constantly putting forward the need for a new building. So he was a happy man in early 1957 when he stood inside the new building, still under construction. But, sadly, he collapsed and died of a heart attack just eight days before it opened.

Wolfgang Gerson

UBC ARCHITECTURE PROFESSOR, Wolfgang Gerson became the first chairman of the Main Source Management Society and left a legacy in the Mount Pleasant neighbourhood that went far beyond the bricks and mortar he laid in his profession. Under his leadership a group of like-minded individuals and community non-profit organizations succeeded in creating affordable rental accommodation in a period of skyrocketing rents. That the groups were able to be self-sufficient in a beautiful old heritage building was great. That the building would also be open to the public was brilliant.

Wolfgang Gerson had been recruited by David Niederauer, another UBC professor, to represent the Greater Vancouver Information and Referral Service on the Main Source Board of Directors. But it wasn't long before the board recognized that Wolfgang would make an excellent chairperson for the society. Roy Crowe was in on the ground floor of the Heritage Hall project and was part of the group who encouraged Wolfgang Gerson's leadership of the managing board. Says Roy, "We needed to get people involved who weren't trying to run an organization. He was

inspirational rather than detail-minded and he gave the project credibility."

Bob Griffiths knew Wolfgang Gerson well. Their friendship developed over home renovation projects and a mutual love of music. It was Wolfgang who convinced Bob to oversee the renovations of Heritage Hall. Bob characterizes him this way: "He was a dynamic and centred kind of person who got the job done. He was a marvellous personality, and a brilliant artist, architect, and musician. If I were to name a mentor, it would be him."

When the Main Source went seeking community input, they recruited the chair of Mount Pleasant's Local Planning Committee, Nancy McKenzie. During the course of the project Nancy had plenty of opportunity to see Wolfgang in action.

"Wolfgang Gerson was the star. He was unrelenting in pestering people and in getting things done, but he was also a very gentle leader. He never took no for an answer, and he could charm the birds out of the trees. There was no hidden agenda with Wolfgang. He just was absolutely single minded about what he wanted, which was the restoration of this building come hell or high water. Wolfgang was wonderful, but he wasn't wacky. He was more nose-to-the-grindstone, just steady going on the project. He led a full and interesting life on his own, with his family and his wife Hilde, and he was very involved in the Unitarian Church, which he designed. I honestly don't believe the project would have got off the ground if it hadn't been for someone like Wolfgang, because he was absolutely neutral. He just kept his eye on the

Wolfgang Gerson and Marguerite Ford take a look at the hole which will house the elevator.
LARRY TROTTER PHOTO

prize. I don't think he was in it for any kind of glory. I think he was very community-minded and absolutely believed in the idea of saving the heritage building and housing the non-profit organizations. I don't think one came before the other in his mind, I think they were so co-mingled."

Susan Baker ultimately became the project architect as well as the creator of the *trompe-l'œil* mural which graces the great room at Heritage Hall. She saw a lot of Wolfgang, particularly during the ornamentation stage of the renovation. "I don't know why he chose this project but it certainly was a wonderful gift because he always had tremendous vision about the possibilities. He was a total optimist. He could see that this could become a centre for this part of the city, and that the space could be turned into a pretty glorious space representing a kind of grand time."

Wally Beck took over the chair when Gerson

stepped down in January 1986, and has his own theory about why Wolfgang was so devoted to the project. "He felt he wanted to repay the community. He was born Jewish in Germany, and was sent off to Britain early on. When in England during the war, he was considered an alien due to his German background and was interned. He eventually came to Canada on a prisoner of war ship and his internment continued here. But Wolfgang still felt very fortunate to have come to Canada. He became highly respected at UBC. I think he wanted to do something that he considered constructive. We were all so impressed by Wolfgang. He was such a moving spirit who worked very quietly and very effectively. He was there during the exciting period of development, and he was the very man for the job."

David Peddle was the Civic Building representative on the Main Source building committee and generally oversaw the renovation process on behalf of the City of Vancouver. Part of that task involved weekly meetings with the building committee, of which Wolfgang was a member. David has perhaps the simplest explanation for Wolfgang's extraordinary dedication to the revitalization of Heritage Hall: "He just seemed to have a love for the building."

After Wolfgang Gerson's death in July, 1991, the main floor was renamed Gerson Hall to honour this extraordinary man. A permanent plaque which acknowledged his leadership and dedication to the project was installed.

CREATING A WORKING STRUCTURE

Because there was a recession going on in Vancouver in 1982-83, there were several professional people who offered free help with the project. Like productive non-profit societies everywhere, the project relied on an amazing corps of volunteers. Their task was to take an old, somewhat decrepit, post office building and turn it into a work space worthy of the heritage name.

In early 1982, the Main Source Management Society was established and the first volunteer Board of Directors was put in place. The structure of the board was set at two representatives from each organization, plus one representative from the Mount Pleasant neighbourhood association. According to Gil Evans it was city alderman Harry Rankin who insisted the board of directors of the society should also include independent community representatives and that the main floor of the building should be reserved for public use. Eventually, Rankin got his way on both suggestions.

In the early days of the restoration, Charles Keast served a short stint as the paid project manager. His job ended shortly after Wolfgang Gerson joined the board of Main Source. Gerson was an architecture professor at UBC and was recruited when it became apparent the project needed leadership from someone with a background in construction and design. As Gil Evans, former executive director of Information Services Vancouver recalls, "When Wolfgang started making plans for the actual renovation, hiring the contractors and so on, he asked Charlie to drop out. I think it is unfortunate that he asked Charlie to leave."

Managing the renovation, while overseen by the City, would be the board's responsibility, as would the building's day-to-day operations and management. Such tasks as creating management structures and working out the details of leases were all tackled with enthusiasm. In December 1982, Chairman Gerson wrote to Max Beck, Director of Social Planning, City of Vancouver: "Our board now has among its 15 members architectural, engineering and planning expertise as well as a group of skilled fundraisers and people that are well acquainted with the cultural needs, concerns and problems with this city. We also have good

> Like productive non-profit societies everywhere, the project relied on an amazing corps of volunteers.

A sample of the brochures, pamphlets and newsletters used to raise funds and increase public awareness of the project.

representation from the two communities of Mount Pleasant and Little Mountain." The group was itching to get started on the restoration, but first they had to raise some money.

FUNDRAISING AND FINAGLING

The building restoration would require a large stack of cash and in the years leading up to Expo 86, economic times were a little tough in Vancouver. Thankfully, City Council had recommended the Society receive capital grants up to $300,000 over the three-year period 1983 –85, subject to Main Source raising the balance of funds necessary to restore the building. This was a figure between $500,000 and $900,000 depending on whose estimates were used as the baseline. And on this project restoration and fundraising were happening at the same time.

The non-profit community groups who made up the Society had years of experience raising funds for their own agencies. They knew how to write noteworthy pitches for government funding. So Main Source was reasonably successful at obtaining grants and loans from various levels of government. Federal job creation grants which, over the years, totaled over $300,000, were very beneficial since labour costs would be one of the biggest project expenses. But job training grants included very little for capital costs and the Society often found itself "labour rich and cash poor." As project architect Susan Baker recalls, "It came together very slowly, because money came together very slowly."

Almost all the money raised came with conditions attached. A $15,000 grant from the Vancouver Foundation was contingent on the Society being able to match the funds. The British Columbia Heritage Trust awarded its maximum $50,000 grant for replacement of the roof. The provincial B.C. Lottery Fund offered $50,000 towards the costs of roofing but this too was contingent on the Society raising the rest of the money to complete the job. And they did it! The Junior League (one of the tenant agencies) awarded its first ever capital grant with $12,000 to be used for the elevator, $5,000 to be used for access for people with disabilities and $3,000 for event expenses on the main floor. The Mount Pleasant Royal Canadian Legion awarded $15,000 to be used for furnishing the main floor.

But going to the general public for funds was largely unsuccessful. This was not due to lack of skill on behalf of the volunteers but rather as former Main Source chairman Wally Beck recalls, "it can be hard to get people to dig into their own pockets." All manner of special events and fundraising schemes were organized. And then there were the detailed (and expensive) recommendations of fundraising consultants and endless brochures, pamphlets, and newsletters to create. Media coverage was solicited to try to raise the public profile of the project. Successful businessman Jimmy Pattison, who owned a large local car dealership, was courted for his support on a number of occasions, but was never enticed into the project.

The City had granted a lot of money to the project, but they also gave a $150,000 loan, which somehow got overspent by almost $40,000. This was a fortunate mistake, otherwise the renovations may never have been finished. In late 1985, board member and accountant, Frank Claassen, negotiated a payback scheme which saw the Society pay the City a $2,225 monthly payment, which included ten percent interest, for the next 12 years. In effect this was very much like a

All manner of special events and fundraising schemes were organized.

mortgage, which, had it been applied for, would likely never have been granted. This loan was fully paid off by March of 1998.

When money was tight it sometimes became difficult to keep the grand scale of the project in mind. But project contractor, Bob Griffiths fondly remembers the enthusiasm of the citizens involved. "They had a common goal and enormous energy for fundraising and grant writing and just a tenacity that would not stop."

THE MAIN FLOOR DEBATE

Philosophical differences about how the coveted main floor space would be used led to some vigorous family feuds. Various proposals saw the space being carved up into office or gallery space. Some wanted it available as performance space for theatre, music and dance. Others saw it as a cultural/multi-ethnic community hall. Some, like the Satellite Video Exchange wanted the space all to themselves. (When Main Source wouldn't agree to this, the video group withdrew from the project.) As work on the main floor progressed, it became clear that the space had the

It took imagination to see the basement as usable space.

potential to offer a community and cultural facility of some kind. In 1983, the Society established the Public Space Council, a committee of the board, to develop plans for the main floor. Members of the local community joined the Council and neighbourhood residents were surveyed for suggestions as to how to best use the space.

The mandate of the Main Source Society, as agreed upon with the City of Vancouver, was for the building to be financially self-supporting. The Society had recognized that proceeds from the rental of the main floor space could help pay operating and renovation costs. But the Society also wanted the building to be a resource to the community. To achieve these goals, the Public Space Council had decided on a business-like three-tier rental structure for the main floor, with the lowest rental rates offered to local community groups and a slightly higher rate to city-wide non-profit groups. Private rentals (weddings, receptions etc.) would pay the highest fees, which, in effect, would subsidize hall use by community groups.

Avenue for the Arts Society (AVA) was formed in 1982 for the express purpose of ensuring local community participation in Main Source. The group joined the Public Space Council and Darlene Nairne, a local resident, put in countless volunteer hours. She was the driving force behind AVA, a group who defined themselves as a society of active visual and performing artists based in the Mount Pleasant/Little Mountain community. AVA wanted to use the building to facilitate cultural activity which would meet the needs of the neighbourhood. AVA wanted to be responsible for programming the main floor and basement space. They proposed an "in-house" group of renters which would include theatre, visual artists, dancers, musicians, craftspeople, writers and the like. These resident groups would get first dibs on the space and would rent any remaining time to touring shows and the general public. They visualized the basement as studio and rehearsal space. They proposed an annual Christmas Craft Fair as one of their ongoing projects and did organize a ten-day event in December, 1983.

The Society recognized that proceeds from the rental of the main floor space could help pay operating and renovation costs.

AVA became full-fledged members of the Main Source Society on
May 4, 1983 and proceeded to try to make their vision come to life.
They planned to move into the basement space and started to negotiate a
lease. It turned out the group had ambitious goals but few financial
assets. They wrote thought-provoking position papers and well thought-
out policy recommendations but it soon became apparent their vision of
what should happen on the main floor was not in tune with the
financial reality of running the building. When it became obvious the
AVA vision was not going to succeed, they accused Main Source of
elitism and of not representing the community. One person who was
involved with Main Source at the time remembers AVA as "extremely
well-intentioned;" another calls them a "royal pain."

On November 19, 1984, Avenue for the Arts was invited to
"withdraw as a member of the Main Source Society." They did not accept
the invitation. In fact things got somewhat nasty. AVA took their
grievances to the press, to federal and civic elected officials and to the
Mount Pleasant Citizen's Planning Committee. Main Source found this
unforgivable since the project everyone had worked so hard to achieve
could have suffered permanent harm from such bad publicity. They also
worried that AVA's agitations and representations would diminish local
support for the restoration project. On January 21, 1985, AVA was
expelled from the Main Source Management Society. Chairman
Wolfgang Gerson's report to the 1985 Annual General Meeting of the
Main Source Society said, "One of the most difficult actions of this year
was the expulsion of one of our members, AVA. It was a decision that
still haunts our Society."

It turned out that
Avenue for the Arts
had ambitious
goals but few
financial assets.

CHAPTER FIVE

The Renovations

A LABOUR OF LOVE

The story of how the building was restored to its stately beauty and put into use as a community facility is a tale of successful collective action. The project would become a labour of love fuelled by a dedication and optimism rarely achieved in a construction project. It's a story best told by some of those who did the work.

Wally Beck was the second chairman of the Main Source Management Society and he remembers his experience as being "always so positive because the first thoughts were how to make Heritage Hall an exciting community building. I was impressed with the talents of the people and their energies, their dedication to the building and its development."

Project architect Susan Baker says the crew that did the work on the building became pretty close. "People became more innovative because it became our project and we felt it belonged to us."

Construction manager Bob Griffiths describes himself as very independent and says that, "working with Heritage Hall gave me the ability to work with a team. There was so much help from the people involved. Everyone had a common goal. They just wanted to make this work so everyone did what he or she did best."

Board member and later building manager Nancy McKenzie is sure she has forgotten about many of the bumps on the restoration road but says she remembers that once the project got started it was like a juggernaut that couldn't be stopped. "Everyone thought it was such a good idea. Yes, of course it could be saved. Yes, of course these agencies should have a place to house themselves. It was a project based in the community, it was not government-led but it came from people who had a true honest interest in improving things for themselves and for others. That's what made it such an admirable project."

60

"People became more innovative because it became our project and we felt it belonged to us."

David Peddle represented the City on the project. Under his watchful eye, the renovations were all done to meet prevailing building codes. "I managed the City's money and reviewed whatever work was done to ensure Main Source was spending the City's money wisely. We directed them so that they didn't mess up on bylaws or problems with the renovations, since we do a lot of renos and they did one."

"David was terrific!" says Susan Baker, "one of those positive people for whom there are only solutions. And even if he said the word problem, he would probably follow it with, 'however, I'm sure we can work something out.'"

The process of saving historic Postal Station C brought people together and made them feel connected to the project and each other. But getting the building in shape was quite a challenge.

Cutting through the concrete from the mezzanine floor in order to build the new back staircase.
LARRY TROTTER PHOTO

FIRST IMPRESSIONS

By the time Roy Crowe, who worked for the Vancouver Volunteer Centre and architect Monty Wood got a look inside the building, it had been empty for five years. The building was in decline. There was spray painting on the outside, and some of the stonework detail was crumbling.

Inside, interesting clues to its former occupants remained. Some, like a "wonderful oak showcase about ten feet long with glass" hinted at its former life as a post office.

Inside, interesting clues to its former occupants remained.

What Roy thought were freezers, "about as large as your living room," were left behind on the second floor by the building's second occupants, the federal Department of Agriculture.

"In the basement there were wooden ballot boxes that had been used at some stage or another in an election," recalls Roy. And, courtesy of the building's last occupant, the RCMP, "about 40 electrical control panels." Then there was the furnace: "It looked like this monster out of the War of the Worlds," laughs Roy. "There are old coal chutes for it along the back lane."

Roy recalls the main floor looking "like a toy house that had the roof pulled off. With its half walls, it was somewhat reminiscent of an old detective's office...with a transom above the door but nothing above that."

The third floor was distinguished by a "sort of wire cage that looked like they'd been keeping chickens in it." All in all, what Roy calls a "rough and ready" place.

On the plus side, "The structural stuff was pretty good," recalls Roy. "When you look at it, you think this is a brick building, but it's not, it's really a reinforced concrete building."

David Peddle agrees that the basic structure of the building was sound. When Heritage Hall became a city property, David represented the City's Civic Buildings department on the Main Source Management Society's Building Committee. According to David "The exterior was pretty solid and it was seismically okay, and met the bylaw pretty well, which is much more than many buildings do. Although it was run

62

down and dirty and hadn't been maintained for a long time, it wasn't in bad condition. A great deal of that project was making a pretty building."

Renovations contractor Bob Griffiths was encouraged to become involved with the project by Main Source board chair Wolfgang Gerson. "He thought it would be right up my alley," says Bob, and he turned out to be right. "I fell in love with the building, too. It's easy to fall in love with that building."

But it wasn't love at first sight.

"The first time I showed up to Heritage Hall it was heartbreaking. You dared not stay in one place for any length of time because the ceiling tiles were falling. It was covered with razor wire, and there had been a lot of vandalism. People had gone in and sprayed the fire extinguishers around, and literally you'd just step aside as these ceiling tiles came dropping down."

However, those were just the superficial problems. The building had been abandoned for some years before Bob saw it, and "definitely needed some tender loving care." Rehabilitating what he calls "a fabulous building" would turn out to be "a little larger job" than he had

The old basement furnace looked like a monster out of *The War of the Worlds.*

The Poop Problem

The war against the pigeons has likely been going on ever since the building opened. The birds have most often been the victors. People who work in the building call them flying rats and consider them a scourge. Buildings like Heritage Hall are vulnerable to pest birds because sheltered niches, crevices and ledges provide ideal nesting and roosting habitats.

When folks first thought about restoring the building in the early 1980s it looked like pigeons were "the master tenants," according to Wally Beck who became the second chairperson of the Main Source Society. "The pigeons really loved Heritage Hall. A lot of our meetings were taken up with how to get rid of the damn pigeons because, of course, they would leave their calling card all over the place."

Once renovations were complete, staff couldn't open their office windows without being exposed to piles of guano, which is a known health hazard. The building had visits from the Workers' Compensation Board and the Environmental Health Division of the City of Vancouver who demanded the problem be cleaned up. Due to the fragile nature of the sandstone, power washing of the building is not allowed. Experts recommend hand washing with soap and a brush, which is a difficult and expensive proposition. Estimates for cleaning always ran into the thousands. Pigeons go back to roost where they are born and so there were always pigeons waiting to mess things up again.

MICHELLE FRAWLEY ILLUSTRATION

Cleaning without solving the poop problem was useless.

Over the last 20 years many deterrents were studied in an effort to get rid of the pests. Hot Foot (which promised not to burn or irritate the feet of birds) was seriously considered until the City of Vancouver vetoed the idea. It had been installed on one City building and they did not "ever want to use it again." Nixilite bird control needle strips were looked at, but since a heavy-duty adhesive which could damage the building was required, this was also outvoted. Tanglefoot, similar to Hotfoot was recommended and discarded. A high frequency noise emitting system invented by someone from the University of Saskatchewan was ordered and installed. It didn't work. Poison feed was used for a while, but humane considerations made that solution unpopular fairly quickly. Rumor had it that the Hotel Vancouver had a resident falcon that kept birds off that ornate building, and unsuccessful attempts were made to somehow attract/rent/borrow one of those. And of course, many suggested rubber snakes and plastic owls. Cats who would live in the building were contemplated, with the hopes they'd patrol the ledges and roofs.

Part of the solution for getting rid of pigeons is to cut off their supply of food. To this day, at least a couple of Main Street business owners regularly feed them on the sidewalks and there are people living in the neighbourhood who feed pigeons as a sort of hobby. Pleas to quit feeding the pests fall on deaf ears. In 1994, building management realized they at least had to clean up the mess. A young mountain climber was hired to rappel his way around the building cleaning ledges.

It was long time board member, David Niederauer who took it upon himself to become a pigeon expert. As a retired professor who enjoyed travel, David even included anti-pigeon research as part of his European adventures. He brought back little sharp pointed plastic cones that had been installed on European heritage building ledges so that pigeons couldn't land. But real success wasn't achieved until David discovered Avian Flyaway, an electric barrier system of bird control. The company, out of Rockwell, Texas promised that "Birds Fly Away & Stay Away." Their system had been used effectively on the Jefferson and Lincoln Memorials and in the summer of 1996, the City of Vancouver paid a couple of Texans to come to Vancouver to install two 115-volt open wire systems on Heritage Hall. The systems are based on Pavlov's theory of behavior modification. The birds are not harmed, but are trained not to land (i.e. they get a little shock if they do).

Of course, it was impossible to wire every inch of the building that a pigeon might find attractive but the system worked well — until it broke down. The City paid for the initial

Staff couldn't open their windows because of the piles of guano on all the ledges.

installation, but left it to the Society to maintain. When the system failed, Heritage Hall had to pay for a man lift, an electrician, and a lift operator. In 1999, that cost $2300. In 2001, another $1400 was required. About one month after the last repair, a pigeon was observed sitting on two eggs on the northwest balcony before she walked onto the wire and flew off. Not a perfect system, but half a dozen pigeons are less troubling than the 200 or so who used to call the building home.

According to Heritage Hall's current board secretary and birding enthusiast Cynthia Crampton, there was a downside to the pigeons moving off the building. With the demise of the pigeons, the rare crested myna also left the area. Cynthia recalls hearing their song over the noise of Main Street traffic. With Vancouver's crested myna population down to five birds, she regrets the loss of their Heritage Hall habitat.

The unique double-sided porcelain fixture in the basement men's washroom was once a lead character in a video titled *Urinalysis*. The video is available at Video In.

66

originally thought. But for Bob, there was an additional attraction: "So many social service agencies were behind it, trying to make it their home."

Susan Baker cut her architectural teeth on Heritage Hall, eventually becoming project architect. She and partner Graham McGarva inherited the renovation job from Downs-Archambault, the firm initially engaged by Wolfgang Gerson on behalf of Main Source. "We saw the building as having great potential," she recalls.

"Everything was kind of overbuilt," enthuses Susan. "It had huge rebar, far more muscular and more of it, and the floors are thick. It's a concrete frame building, which has brick and stone on the outside, infilled with brick paneling. It's heavy, and it's got a big, pretty much square floor plate. So it's got a very stable kind of form here in the earthquake zone."

Upon inspection, the only flaw Susan remembers had been caused by a creek which had run diagonally beneath the building. The concrete in the basement had cracked, showing the very line of the subsidence over many, many, years, but the walls remained unaffected.

"There was no cracking in the walls. Everything was as solid as the day it was built, so we were able to remove walls rather than have to build a lot of special adaptations to bring it up to seismic code."

The urinal found in the men's basement washroom still makes Susan smile, "I can remember our excitement. It's a one piece with two places to stand. Maybe it was an industrial fitting that post offices used in those days, but it's kind of a neat thing. There's nothing like that in the women's washroom."

GETTING STARTED

Main Source decided to first concentrate on the main floor of the building. It was hoped events held in a restored main floor would attract public attention which would lead to support for the overall project. Work really got underway when Main Source obtained federal government job creation grants. Project

Preparing the main
ballroom for floor tiles.
KAREN CHRISTIANSEN PHOTO

67

architect Susan Baker recalls, "The biggest gift was the manpower grant which gave us the labour which is always the biggest cost in a project. As architects, Baker and McGarva were responsible for providing information to Bob as the contractor who would then supervise the young manpower workers he was training onsite. An engineer would check anything that was structural."

For Bob, the "gift" of semi-skilled labour was sometimes a mixed blessing. But when members of the crew did take the project to heart, the results were gratifying. Susan remembers Bob's patience in training people. "Everybody did different stuff from what their usual skill set was. It gave at least a dozen people a kind of marginal income for a period of time, and I really think that lots of skills were learned."

Mark Ryyppo was one project worker whom Bob and Susan both remember well.

"I think of him as an artist," says Bob. "He was able to undertake almost any task and would study the job at hand and become quite proficient at it. Some of the others had some idiosyncrasies that made it difficult to create a harmonious workforce, but Mark was pretty constant."

Karl the Custodian

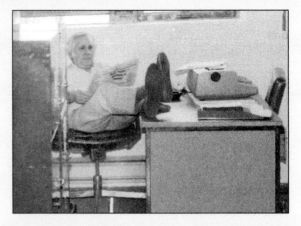

Karl Caskenette, who worked at Heritage Hall as a caretaker from 1985-93 left his mark on the hearts and minds of all those he worked with. He came in as a construction worker and stayed to provide maintenance in the building he had helped renovate. He is remembered for his careful attention to the physical plant of the building, for his ability to encourage social cohesion, and for the caring way he used his cooking abilities.

Roy Crowe was working with Volunteer Vancouver, one of the agencies which moved into the building once the office space was finished. For him, Karl was a constant in the operation. "He was the one who provided a certain amount of glue for the building. He started as a kind of custodian, but he played a much bigger role. He wasn't overly zealous about cleaning and fixing, but he put on parties about once a month down in the hall where we would chip in a buck or two and have a little lunch for all the staff and volunteers. It brought everybody in the building together. He worked on getting the third floor roof deck fixed up and it was called Karl's Bistro in his memory."

Nancy McKenzie has her own memories of times with Karl. In addition to sitting on the board and board committees, Nancy also spent time managing Heritage Hall, and that meant working closely with Karl. " Karl did things in his own way, but he felt so protective of the building. He was the guru of the building who knew every inch and idiosyncratic thing. Karl fancied himself a cook, so we would have these Friday afternoon lunches. We'd do the food so people could come together and get to know each other. When we finished the roof deck upstairs they became elaborate barbecue affairs. That was a lot of fun, and I think that was a really successful way of giving people who worked in the same building a chance to get together."

Wally Beck, who chaired the board during the latter part of the renovations, had this to say: "Karl was our first permanent maintenance guy in the place, and if you wanted to know what was going on in the building, he knew. He was very loyal, and did over and above what he was expected to do, or paid to do."

Bob Griffiths who managed the construction project got to know Karl very well, and saw him on a regular basis until Karl's death at age 68 in 1993. "Sadly he went very quickly so I was not there at his death, but we were close enough that I wanted to be. I certainly visited him at the hospice and always remember fondly all of our times at Heritage Hall."

"Karl was a no-nonsense kind of guy who always did his job and was completely dedicated. He just had street smarts and I was able to take his advice on handling some of the more outrageous employees at the time."

Susan worked closely with Mark on the restoration of the main hall. "There didn't seem to be anything that Mark didn't know how to do. He was a very good photographer, a man of few words, but with a really good mind. He invented a means of making the mouldings which I was designing."

"Wolfgang Gerson wanted ornaments to make the room into a great hall, so we took the industrial mouldings which were already around the columns, and in some places bits of moulding on the walls and around doorways. Mark made moulds of architectural details and then cast plaster copies."

Mark Ryyppo was a master at creating architectural detail out of plaster.
LARRY TROTTER PHOTOS

He installed these details by taking wet plaster castings and holding them up in exactly the right place on the wall. They didn't have any particular structural strength, but when they dried they became like one solid piece.

"This was brilliant. We could do anything. We started by repairing some of the details which had been knocked off when partitions had been built. We fixed those, and then it was sort of like 'eureka,' we could really go to town on this."

69

Exterior rosettes were replicated for interior detailing. This is on the main floor ceiling.
DOUGLAS KENNEDY PHOTO

"Wolfgang would ask questions like, 'Could we maybe have a rim that went around here and pull this together?' So I'd draw up a full scale drawing of the moulding in sections, Mark would make a casting for this moulding, produce the moulding, and put it on."

"In a funny way, this was right up there with old craftsmen abilities, working on cathedrals and casting themselves as apostles and sticking themselves over the door," she laughs. "We didn't do that but we could have done all kinds of things like that."

"What we did was take the rosettes from the entrance to the building and cast them and then put them on the columns, and then put nice mouldings around so the place started to look like a French country chateau, instead of what I call the industrial chateau look that it had originally."

"The fancy bits made in plaster weren't like Adam's friezes with dripping folds of fabric. They were kind of brutal and coarse. They still have this big cornice run around, and dentils which would also be quite crude and coarse in grain. Then there would be a tassel that was straight, kind of an industrial motif, suitable for a post office, which was the original intention for the building."

Creating architectural details out of plaster was just one of the good things that Susan maintains came out of not having quite enough money. Other economical, though equally inventive solutions made a real impact on the appearance of the main hall.

"The most inexpensive flooring material available is vinyl asbestos tile, so we created this beautiful patterned floor which completely lends itself to the look of the room. We also found out from an acoustical expert that we could get away with a small amount of an extremely absorbing acoustical material on the ceiling. We put it in a pattern on the ceiling to match the pattern of tiles on the floor, and then we hung a big light fixture in the middle. That went a long way to keeping the hall from being just one big reverberating sound box."

The restoration of the stained glass skylight which had originally been located at the top of the main staircase added another classy touch to the main floor. The skylight was taken off site to be restored. It became an extravagant ceiling light cover in front of the elevator. Other window glass and the main floor chandeliers were matched to the gold coloured glass. The staircase skylight was filled in with plain window glass.

Unfortunately, the large window on the second floor south side of the building didn't fare as well. Susan Baker explains: "It had to be removed because of fire regulations. When they built Heritage Hall, there weren't any tall buildings near it." The removal of this window took away a source of fresh air cross ventilation for the second floor offices and created the need for expensive ventilation systems which could have been avoided if the window had been left in place.

The building is heated by hot water radiators and these were painted gold to make them look spiffy, curtains were put up, and the entire place was spruced up with an elaborate paint job.

The washroom on the main floor was renovated to make it wheelchair accessible. "We took out the partitions to make it a single room," recalls Susan. "I think it's the original sink in the corner. I know it well because I washed many brushes in there. It also has wonderful

Tassels, an original rather industrial decorative touch, were highlighted with gold paint.
DOUGLAS KENNEDY PHOTO

The almost finished main floor. Only the stained glass skylights and chandeliers are missing.

white tile. It seems to me that I actually got out the elbow grease and went at that tile myself. I didn't want to get rid of it because it has so much character."

But some of the problems in the building could not be solved with the relatively simple application of decorative touches, elbow grease, or paint.

REPLACING THE ROOF

Problems with the roof had been identified as early as 1977 in a building analysis done by Public Works Canada. The report noted, "Some slates are missing, and many have been dislodged and are host to moss or other vegetation.. The roof is highly ornamental, and the colour and patterns of the slate are very important to the total effect." In order to maintain the integrity of the building, it was thought important to replace the tiles with a type and colour of tiles similar to those installed back in 1916 . Wolfgang Gerson summarized what he knew about the roof: "A.C. Hope's plans of 1913 called for a white asbestos roofing. Later plans identify 'glass slate' as the preferred material, depicted in the architectural drawings as being laid in a regular shingle pattern. Neither of these materials were actually applied. The roofing in place in the spring of 1983 was long thought to be glass slate on account of its glazed surface, but was in reality red asbestos, laid in diamond format".

When it was decided in 1984 that all the roof tiles needed to be replaced, there were very few roofing companies who would even consider such a job. But Coast Hudson, a local company was up for the challenge. First Main Source had to raise over $150,000 to pay for the job.

Even though professional roofers eventually did the work, Main Source project staff had to make sure the job was done to specifications and that meant going out on the roof.

Bob Griffiths admits to being afraid of heights. "After the roof was re-done, I had to get up there as part of my job, to inspect what the roofers had done." The only way to get on the roof from inside the building is to climb up to the top level of the clock tower, haul yourself through a trapdoor, climb another ladder, open one more hatch and find yourself at the base of the flagpole. From there you can climb out onto the roof. Says Bob, "I got up there and realized I was way out of my element, frightened, and I literally hugged the flag pole because I thought I was going to fall for sure. It's a very steep roof, very high, and the traffic is going by down below and that creates another diversion."

"After quite a few minutes of hugging the flag pole I finally lowered myself over the edge to look at some of the caulking details. That's something I would not want to do again."

Susan Baker also made a trip up to the roof. She says, "I wish I had a picture of me

Intricate scaffolding was required to repair the steeply pitched roof.

The Clock, the Bell and the Tower

IN ALL OF VANCOUVER, only one hand-wound tower clock remains. That unique clock ticks atop Heritage Hall, as it has done for nearly eight decades of the building's 85-year history.

Each week on the same day, at the same time, one of the members of Chapter 121 of the National Association of Watch and Clock Collectors (NAWCC) climbs the tower to wind the clock. He has a one-hour window of time in which to do the job. He makes his way up the tower's 45 stairs to the clock room, gives the clock's crank 112 turns, winding the cables to lift the heavy counterweights up the tower to begin their next slow downward passage, which will keep the clock ticking and the bell chiming for

another week. NAWCC member Don Ourum has been helping to maintain the clock for many years. Don likes to compile statistics. In the 79 years the clock has been operating, Don figures 184,860 stairs have been climbed. The crank has been turned 637,728 times. Pretty impressive numbers! Almost as impressive as the figures the clock itself has mounted up. Number of hammer strokes to the bell: four million. Number of beats of the pendulum: two thousand million.

The clock was built in about 1914 or 1915 by J. B. Joyce & Co. of Whitchurch, Shropshire, England. This long-established company traces its origins back to 1690 and is now a part of the Smith of Derby Group.

In the days of live-in caretakers, maintaining the clock, winding it and making sure it kept accurate time was a part of the caretaker's job. The last caretaker continued to look after it for a short

while after moving out. During the RCMP tenancy, there was a maintenance person who took a particular interest in the clock. Reg Chase of the RCMP remembers, "There was a tall blond Swiss fellow who used to service the clock. He had serviced clock bells in Europe, and he said this was one of the best built clocks that he'd ever seen. He said it would last for a hundred years if it was maintained properly…and he said that the bell had a tone that was second-to-none."

When the RCMP, the last of the building's federal occupants, left the building in 1976, the clock sat idle for seven years. Then in 1983, the NAWCC came to the rescue. Clocks are a passion for the members of this group and over time they restored the clock to its original condition. It was a big job for volunteers to tackle, but they put in a tremendous amount of work which included cleaning, fixing and painting the interior of the tower. Chapter 121 has made the clock their special project. In 2000 and 2001, volunteer extraordinaire Jim Marinello put together a team to give the clock a facelift, or, more accurately, four whole new faces. Each

clock face is made up of scores of pieces of leaded opaque white glass. Over the decades some pieces of glass had cracked and the caulking was starting to disintegrate. The volunteers painstakingly cut and replaced each and every piece of glass.

In exchange for monthly meeting space and a little storage space in the Heritage Hall basement, the men of Chapter 121 take wonderful care of the clock. They maintain it with the kind of dedication and pride it is impossible to buy.

The gleaming clock gears are visible through a glass fronted cabinet up in the tower.
DOUGLAS KENNEDY PHOTOS

Tall Tales and Local Legends

MYTH Little Ben, the Heritage Hall clock, was built by the J.B. Joyce & Co., the same company that built Big Ben.

REALITY They do appear similar, but the J.B. Joyce & Co. didn't build Big Ben.

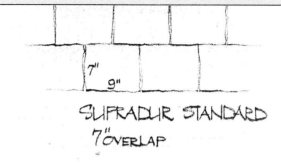

EQUAL FACET

SUPRADUR STANDARD
7" OVERLAP

Title	SLATE ROOF PATTERNS	Jobsite Inst. Ref No.		Sketch No.
		Scale 1/4" = 3"		
		Drawn SPJ		SKA 19
Project	MAIN SOURCE	Date JUNE 15/83		
		Downs/Archambault. Architects		

Above Architectural sketch showing options for roof tile replacement. *Below* The heights and angles of the roof makes maintenance extremely challenging.
DOUGLAS KENNEDY PHOTO

sitting up on that bloody roof. I want you to know that the only architect who stood on that roof was me. Graham McGarva wasn't going up there for love nor money, and Wolfgang Gerson, I'll bet you it wouldn't even cross his mind."

"You know how steep that roof is? I had to go and climb up the valley that runs between the main roof that runs north and this little roof that comes out and runs east/west from the bell tower. I had to go up and inspect the tile. It was quite a thrill."

"I had never been afraid of heights before, but I'll tell you, sitting up there I certainly was thinking about it."

The roofers of course, had to find a safer way to work at such heights and angles. The scaffolding they erected surrounded the entire building and created a visually dramatic sight.

Having scaffolding provided an opportunity to give the outside of the building a complete cleaning and once-over. The building could not be power washed since water under pressure takes the surface off old brick, rendering it more vulnerable. And the sandstone would simply flake off if exposed to water with any force behind it. "The washing of the building was very low tech," laughs Bob. "We had a lot of people on all levels of that scaffolding, with buckets and little scrub brushes, sometimes even toothbrushes, because we couldn't just go in there and pressure wash it."

THE ELEVATOR

Setting a new hydraulic elevator in place wasn't far behind the roof in terms of expense and difficulty of installation. There had been an old industrial elevator which proved very useful during construction, but a new hydraulic elevator was required for disabled access. This proved to be the most daunting task in the entire undertaking.

In a report to the 1983 membership meeting of the Junior League, Vicki Hyndman had this to say about the elevator. "Because this is a heritage building we cannot put a penthouse on the top of the roof to house the elevator shaft like most apartment buildings and office buildings do. Therefore we have to drill down 45 feet through the earth's surface on the bottom in order to prepare for the installation of the hydraulic system to work the elevator. The elevator will cost us $85,000. We do not have those funds as yet: however we have done the preparatory work of drilling 45 feet at a cost of $15,000. We felt it necessary to do the preparatory work before the main floor was finished. We had to remove the front doors in order to get the drilling rig in and

Left Punching through the concrete in preparation for the construction of the new back staircase.
Below It was necessary to drill 45 feet into the ground to prepare for the installation of the elevator. Looking down into the elevator excavation from the main floor.
LARRY TROTTER PHOTOS

to have done it after the main floor was opened would have been duplicating costs and been an inefficient use of time and money."

According to Bob Griffiths, "The elevator was an enormous project, very difficult and very expensive. We had to cut many holes in the floor." A secondary stairwell was to become the new elevator's shaft but "the building was built out of plumb so we had to cut vertically through concrete walls to make room for this thing to go in."

"The building was like a parallelogram. Each individual wall might have been close to vertical, but it didn't necessarily follow that the walls lined up." Because of the time that it was built, different crews apparently worked on different floors of the building. "One crew built the first floor, and then the second crew would build the second floor, and so on. It became abundantly clear that some of the workers back then had a better ability at the trade than others."

WATER LEAKS

Of all the things that can go wrong with an aging heritage building, water leaks and flooding are probably the most challenging problems. Heritage Hall had more than its fair share of leaks with many of them caused by clogged or leaky down-spouts and eaves.

"There was and may still be a nasty water problem because the drains went through the walls that emptied the roof of its water," according to Bob. "There were constantly bulges in walls and paint blistering and water running down and mould growths and things, but I believe that's all worked out now," he says optimistically.

Roy Crowe remembers how "the walls on the north side just poured with water in the early years. I don't know how many times we had to pull up all the carpets and dry them out."

THE DREADED ASBESTOS

It wasn't too surprising that asbestos had been used in a variety of the original building materials. There was suspicion that insulation around basement pipes contained the dreaded asbestos and City testing confirmed that hunch. The choice was to remove the offending material

Of all the things that can go wrong with an aging heritage building, water leaks and flooding are probably the most challenging problems.

or to cover it up. The City recommended removal. Prices for removal and re-insulation ranged from $18,000 to $35,000. A consultant hired by the City greatly reduced the price and scope of the asbestos removal down to about $10,000.

In the end, the primary site of asbestos problems was in the ducts and around the boilers and according to Bob Griffiths, removing it wasn't that difficult. "Asbestos is quite stable as long as it's not disturbed, so we only had to stabilize the parts that could be bumped and release particles into the air."

Nonetheless, when the City put the job out to tender, it turned out to be "really expensive, high end. They were talking about separate chambers, and they would

Bob Griffiths leads a tour of skylights and staircases.
LARRY TROTTER PHOTO

have portable showers, and they would come out with these sort of space suit type things, but in reality, when the contract was finally let, there were all these guys in t-shirts with cigarettes rolled into their sleeves," laughs Bob. "It was like something out of the 1950s."

As City of Vancouver employee David Peddle puts it, "Perhaps we would have found more asbestos now because we do more fiddling around with it. There probably would have been asbestos in the floor tile and perhaps in some of the fire stone, but we weren't involved in identifying it then with the vigour we do nowadays."

MORE LOVE THAN MONEY

Moving from one phase of the restoration to the next always depended on whether or not adequate money had been raised. At times this made the planning and scheduling of work next to impossible.

Bob Griffiths explains, "There was always this threat of imminent shut down. You'd just poured your heart and soul into this thing, and it

Opening Day

FIXING UP THE grand room on the main floor of the building took priority over the restoration of the basement and the second and third floors. Even though providing new office space to the non-profit agencies was the prime motivation for the project, it was decided to get the main floor up and running since its availability as a public rental space would hopefully attract interest and raise funds for the overall project.

The opening was held November 20, 1983. As he was wont to do, Chairman Wolfgang Gerson delivered an eloquent speech to the hundreds of people who attended the event. He said, "In spite of leaking roofs and other blemishes outside, our Board decided to put all our forces and funds into the completion of the main floor, this grand space, so that it could be the first part open to the public and make itself known as the Main Cultural Centre in the heart of the city."

Heritage Hall's transformation was indeed startling considering the condition the building had been in prior to its restoration. On opening day Mayor Mike Harcourt told a reporter, "Let me put it this way… The building could have been used as a setting for a horror movie. There were creaking doors and floors, leaky pipes, dangerous stairs and all the other ingredients for a horror house when we visited about a year ago."

Board member, Nancy McKenzie recalls opening day, "In some ways it was kind of like giving up your baby. It had been our (those involved with rebuilding and redecorating the room) playground, we had free reign and then after the official opening it became everyone's. I had expected maybe two or three hundred people but we had thousands of people come through. It was hilarious, people were very interested in it."

With the opening of the main floor rental space, the dream of restoring the building to a useful community resource was one step closer to reality.

Above The local press were excited about the building restoration project.
Below Mayor Michael Harcourt hands out souvenir plaster rosettes at the opening day ceremonies.

Buy a Share Campaign

THE SALE OF Honorary Shares was one of the more creative methods Main Source dreamed up to raise capital for renovating the building. For a $100 tax-deductible donation the shareholder got a fancy, individually numbered gold-stamped certificate signed by the mayor of the day, Michael Harcourt. The fundraising scheme was thought up by well-known Vancouver developer Andre Molnar, who took time off from building stylish condominiums to help raise funds to restore Heritage Hall. Honorary Share number one went to Elsie Hudson, a Mount Pleasant resident who bid $725 for the privilege. On that day in February, 1985, Mrs. Hudson was on her way to pick up her vacuum cleaner from a repair shop when she "saw these fellas standing in front of Heritage Hall. They were all dressed up like Beefeaters…Usually I just walk by, but they really made me curious, so I just followed them in." Mrs. Hudson surprised everyone with her generous bid.

Mayor Michael Harcourt left, Andre Molnar right.

just looked like it wasn't going to get finished. It seemed you were always just standing on one foot waiting to see what could come of the next grant, or how we could make it work, or where money was coming from. I think that was probably the worst for me. There were no real disasters, with so many untrained people working outside their normal vocation, there were still no injuries, no real sad stories. I am patient. If I hadn't been, the project might have fallen apart. There were always these little peaks and valleys."

Susan Baker agrees. "The lack of money made the project stall so much. My time painting the mural bridged some of that time when there wasn't much happening. There was a core of people to do the work, but sometimes no money. Those were low times."

It's a familiar story to Roy Crowe. "We were always looking for money. We had to pay for an elevator and all kinds of things that were never in the original building like the back staircase, which was required for fire code."

"And the (clock) tower had to be reinforced," adds Roy. "Now there are big heavy beams in the tower to prevent crumbling." On the up side,

82

A series of haunting and humorous faces grace the west and north sides of the building. No two are alike.
DOUGLAS KENNEDY PHOTO

the repair and maintenance of the clock in the tower was undertaken in exchange for monthly meeting space on the main floor by the National Association of Watch and Clock Collectors (Chapter 121), whose members continue to ensure its smooth operation to this day.

Nancy McKenzie was one of those constantly on the lookout for funding and freebies. She was also the one who eventually came up with the rental scheme for the main hall which would allow more funds to flow to Main Source coffers.

"The idea was that eventually the tenants wouldn't have to pay rent, just operating expenses, but that's a hard one to do," muses Nancy. "We were lucky to get the Vancouver Little Theatre as a basement tenant because the basement was not that usable, and it worked out well for them. The only problem was when there were weddings and dances on Saturday night and it was noisy. I think they were unbelievably forbearing to be able to operate a theatre space under those conditions. It didn't hurt that the Vancouver Little Theatre came with its own trust fund set up after the sale of the New York Theatre on Commercial Drive. "They had money to put into their projects," according to Roy Crowe.

In-kind contributions helped to stretch meagre funds. "We were shameless when it came to free stuff," says Nancy McKenzie. Things like a promotional magazine, written and designed by journalism students from Langara College, *faux* marbling (for the stairway to the second floor), and trade-offs with the clock society. "We were cheap," she laughs, "we had to be, there was no money.

It took a few years and a lot of experimenting for the Society to hit

Deciding which space went to which group required many meetings, lots of discussion and some jockeying for position.

83

Detail of the hand-painted main floor vault door.
DOUGLAS KENNEDY PHOTO

on a successful formula for renting out the main hall, "We realized we weren't a community centre. It was an interesting evolution to realize it was not our responsibility to program the space. It wasn't something we were particularly good at," according to Nancy. A public space committee set policy and decided on a three-tier rental policy which gave local and community groups preferential pricing

MOVING IN

Work on the second and third floors went on throughout 1984 and '85. This was to become the new office space for the four non-profit tenant agencies. Deciding which space went to which group required many meetings, lots of discussion and some jockeying for position. Among other things, the tenant agencies had to think about ceiling acoustics, floor coverings, wall coverings, location of partitions, choice and location of lighting, reception desk locations, telephone connections, and sharing space.

The non-profit organizations moved into their newly constructed office space in November, 1985.

Ron Kowalski, one of the volunteers who maintain the Heritage Hall clock, gets ready to put in the final piece of replacement glass.

Roy Crowe recalls, "They did a good job. The building was all polished up and painted and carpeted." However, there were what he calls "a few little funnies," like the decision that garage insulation was a really interesting treatment for ceilings. "It was a cheap way to cover the concrete and deaden the sound. The only thing is that it kept falling off, so you'd be at a meeting and these little white bits would come floating through the air like feathers, and people would say, 'Ewww, is that asbestos?'" Roy laughs. "It was just plain old cellulose, but it had to go."

Nancy McKenzie agrees, calling the spray stuff on the ceiling "the biggest disaster, a tactical error because we didn't have enough money to deal with soundproofing, and had bad fortune in choosing something inappropriate."

Neighbourhood residents know the time thanks to the four illuminated clock faces and the big bell which chimes hourly between 9 a.m. and 9 p.m.
DOUGLAS KENNEDY PHOTO

The Mural

When the great hall on the main floor was nearing completion, it became apparent that the room would benefit from some kind of focal point. Chairman Wolfgang Gerson thought about commissioning an art student to paint a mural on the east wall of the room. But project architect Susan Baker decided this was a project she'd like to tackle herself. So for three and a half months she became a muralist.

The mural Susan chose to execute employs an ancient technique called *trompe l'œil*, which literally means "to fool the eye." The magic of the technique is to suggest a window or other architectural feature where none actually exists. Susan decided to pull architectural elements from the building into the mural and also to pull the neighbourhood in and put it on the wall. She propped her feet on the railing of the third floor balcony and did a very careful drawing of the Mt. Pleasant neighbourhood to the east of Heritage Hall with the mountains in the distance.

Fellow worker Mark Ryyppo managed to take a photograph of the mountains one morning before the smog got too thick and Susan used the photograph to put the mountains on the mural as accurately as they would appear on a clear day.

Of course, Susan admits to exercising some artistic license. "If anyone ever notices, I moved Mount Baker into Canada," Susan laughs. "It has always been on the edge of the visual plane when you're looking at that view but if I had been strictly honest I was going to have Golden Ears (which is in Maple Ridge) naturally in the picture. Then Mount Baker was going to have to be just a foothill, and I didn't want that to

happen. So I distorted a few things and moved Central Park into the plane and put Mount Baker over there as well, and it gave me a left and a right plane to my view of the sky."

Susan also played around with the use of colour. She maintains, "You don't have to do a photo mural for people, in fact that would not be interesting, because a photo mural would have been very grey."

"I took the colours of the building, the red of the brick, the rose marble which is a composite marble (a younger marble not quite on its way to true marble and the reason you can see that is because it has all those creatures in it), and another older marble that was a russet colour, a very rich brownish red, one of my very favourite colours, a good industrial colour, sort of like primer red." Susan also incorporated the colour of the floor tiles, "which were ochre, a kind of Edwardian green with a fair amount of grey and yellow in it, not much blue if any. When I looked out over the balustrade at Mount Pleasant, I saw all those colours. The painting has the colours from the building expanded into the colours of Mount Pleasant as a predominant palette. I decided to set October as the date of the mural and we were into some beautiful autumn colour and that was also integrated. That's one of the reasons the mural is as handsome as it is."

Susan decided to use house paint as her basic medium. "Latex acrylic is very absorbent — once it goes on the wall it dries pretty fast — you have to work quickly, but it's forgiving, you can fix mistakes. It had maybe three coats of primer on it, tinted into the colours that were going to be in those areas, and the sky is a full *trompe-l'œil*, which is to say it probably has 75 layers of colour from the bottom to the top because it gets lighter where you go up to the top of the sky, in this particular case to make the eye flow up."

Workers on the restoration project got to know each other quite well. Susan depicted various people who had worked on the

MARK RYYPPO PHOTOS

restoration project as little figures on the mural. Says Susan, "Bob Griffiths, our construction manager is seen taking out the garbage. And Joe Horvath, the painter, is on a bicycle. Shauna McGovern, our public relations person, is also there with her very curly carroty red hair."

Overall Susan Baker was "very pleased with the outcome of the mural. It looked like impressionist work."

Her mural, which captured a view of the neighbourhood that existed two decades ago, is now becoming its own bit of Mount Pleasant history.

CHAPTER SIX

Who's Upstairs?

A tour through Heritage Hall's second- and third-floor tenant agencies provides a glimpse into the way that community social services have developed in British Columbia over the last century. All the agencies have been around for decades, and all have changed with the times. The fact they all remain tenants in 2002 proves that the original idea of housing them in the building was a good one.

THE ASSOCIATION OF NEIGHBOURHOOD HOUSES

The Association of Neighbourhood Houses (ANH) is one of the oldest corporations in the province of British Columbia. It proudly holds registration number 36. It was in 1894 that ANH, under the name Alexandra Non-Sectarian Orphanage and Children's Home, began its legacy of providing social services in greater Vancouver. By 1938, the former Children's Home had become the first Neighbourhood House in the province.

> The fact they all remain tenants in 2002 proves that the original idea of housing them in the building was a good one.

The Association's mission is "to improve and enhance the quality of family and neighbourhood life in our communities." The member houses and camps provide programs and services to individuals, families and community groups to meet the particular needs of each community.

A lot of number crunching goes on in the second floor ANH Central Service offices in Heritage Hall. Staff in the Finance Department do the payroll and record keeping for 370 employees each year. They also help with budget preparation and financial reporting for all the House/Units. Support and administrative services, as well as human resource issues and promotion of the Association are all dealt with through these offices.

Each month about three thousand people make use of the lower mainland neighbourhood houses. With over 100 years experience, the

association knows how to make neighbourhoods better places to live, and remains dedicated to that goal.

INFORMATION SERVICES VANCOUVER

To many people, Information Services Vancouver is synonymous with the Red Book, so prominent is this major directory of social services. Started in 1953 as a service of the Community Chest and Councils (later renamed the United Way of the Lower Mainland) the Community Information Service (CIS) was first housed in United Way offices. Funded by the Rotary Club and the Junior League, CIS initially provided information on health, welfare and related services and later expanded to cover the entire range of community services. The first directory of services, forerunner of the Red Book, was published in 1958.

In 1973 the CIS became a service of the Crisis Intervention and Suicide Prevention Centre of Greater Vancouver and the name was changed to Community Information Centre (CIC). In 1977 CIC became an independent agency called the Greater Vancouver Information and Referral Service. The first computer system was purchased in 1980 and the advantages of automation in the field of

The Association of Neighbourhood Houses began its legacy of providing social services as the Alexandra Non-Sectarian Orphanage and Children's Home.

information and referral soon became apparent.

The name of the agency was changed one last time in 1985 to Information Services Vancouver. This was the same year the agency moved into Heritage Hall.

VANCOUVER VOLUNTEER CENTRE

This thriving agency began life in 1943 as the Central Volunteer Bureau of Vancouver. When the Canadian Government War Services Department put out a call for women to assist in the war effort, the response was immediate and enthusiastic. By the conclusion of the war, the program could boast 10,000 active volunteers.

The group, renamed the Women's Voluntary Service, set up their first office in two rooms in a downtown office building at a monthly rent of $20. The first budget was a whopping $170 per month which included a $100 monthly salary for an executive director. Funding was raised by donations and was greatly assisted by the Junior League's initial donation of $2,500. Volunteers concentrated on developing Block Plans which would enable women to work in their own homes in the company of neighbours to provide clothing and other necessities to war victims. They also developed child care centres where children from England could be sheltered until suitable placement in private homes could be located.

With the war grinding down the agency went through a reorganization. In June, 1945 the need for a permanent Volunteer Bureau was identified and in 1946 the Community Chest accepted the Bureau as a member agency. In its first post-war year of service the Bureau placed volunteers in charity agencies throughout the city and continued to collect clothing and food packages to send to people in Europe.

Over the next six decades the Volunteer Bureau worked hard to find "the right volunteers for the right situation." During the 1950s and '60s, the challenge was to match volunteers with needy agencies. In the 1950s, board members successfully recruited students as volunteers and also took over Volunteers for Seniors, a program initiated by the Junior

Over the next six decades the Volunteer Bureau worked hard to find "the right volunteers for the right situation."

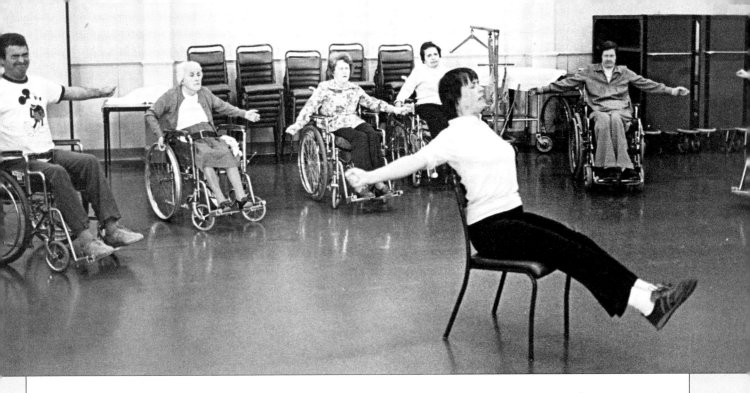

League of Vancouver, which sent volunteers to nursing and boarding homes to add variety and stimulation to the lives of seniors. By 1964 volunteers associated with the Bureau contributed 28,000 hours to the community.

The Volunteer Bureau changed its name to the current Vancouver Volunteer Centre in 1978 and its function was redefined to include training as well as recruitment of volunteers. In the '80s, the Centre was a catalyst for the creation of community college and university extension courses in volunteer and non-profit management.

JUNIOR LEAGUE OF GREATER VANCOUVER

Perhaps the grandmother of all voluntary organizations, the Junior League of Greater Vancouver celebrated its 70th anniversary in 2001. This woman- led organization strives to improve the community through the effective action and leadership of trained volunteers. The League's purpose is exclusively educational and charitable and its list of accomplishments since 1931 is staggering.

The Hamper Project, which provides basic domestic necessities for women about to leave shelters, and Backpacks for Kids, which provides school supplies for children in need, are two of the most recent League projects. One to One, a children's literacy program started by the League in 1992 has become so successful that this year a separate society was formed. The One to One program trains volunteer tutors to go into

The Vancouver Volunteer Centre works to match those willing to volunteer with those who need volunteer help.

Junior League members
circa 1950.
CANADIAN PACIFIC RAILWAY PHOTO

The list of
Junior League
accomplishments
since 1931 is
staggering.

Vancouver schools to provide tutoring to children in primary and
intermediate grades.

The League has a history of getting projects up and running
successfully. They were co-founders of Science World, and founders of
the Community Arts Council and the Vancouver Volunteer Centre.
They have been instrumental in such successful projects as Elizabeth
Fry Group Living Home, Children's Hospital Library, Feeling Yes,
Feeling No Sexual Abuse Education Program, the Red Cross Family
Support Service Prevention Program, Jericho School for the Deaf
Program, and many other health or social service related programs.

The League has also supported cultural activities working with First
Night Celebration of the Arts, Vancouver Symphony Society, the
Vancouver Art Gallery, and Theatre Terrific.

The Junior League Thrift Shop on East Broadway sells clothing,
household goods, toys and the like to discriminating second-hand
shoppers in the Mount Pleasant neighbourhood. Proceeds from the shop
help support the Junior League volunteer initiatives as do such exciting
fundraising events as Home and Garden Tours and World Affairs
Dinners.

With almost 400 members, the Junior League is looking forward to
many more years of developing the potential of women volunteers.

GONE BUT NOT FORGOTTEN

VANCOUVER LITTLE THEATRE ALLIANCE The VLTA was established in 1921 and is the oldest amateur theatre organization in North America. The VLTA developed community theatre with opportunities for amateurs to perform and perfect their skills. The group once had 2,000 members and its own theatre, the York on Commercial Drive. Many who came through the ranks of the VLTA went on to work in professional theatre. Actors and performers like Dave Broadfoot, Bruno Gerussi, Don Francks, Otto Lowy, Jane Mortifee, Chief Dan George, Jessie Richardson, Jeff Hyslop, Pia Shandel and an almost endless list of others were involved with the VLTA.

The non-profit group moved into the basement of Heritage Hall in 1984. Vancouver Little Theatre acted as a venue for new professionals. They also offered acting, film and voice technique classes, actors' workshops, and audition and rehearsal space. Over time, VLTA evolved into a theatrical resource board rather than a production house. What this meant is that VLTA rented out space to others wanting to put on small-scale live theatre. Vancouver Little Theatre occupied the modest basement space until 2001 and over the 17 years many, many exciting and memorable performances were mounted. Much of the work presented in the Little Theatre was being seen in Vancouver for the first time.

THE WRITERS' UNION OF CANADA Until they moved out in 2001, this western regional office of The Writers' Union had the distinction of renting the smallest office in Heritage Hall. Since 1984, they occupied a tiny third floor space which rented for $67 a month at its highest rate. But the aims of this organization were never low. The union exists to advance writers' interests and to address such issues as copyright law, censorship, literacy and cultural funding cuts.

Much of the work presented in the Little Theatre was being seen in Vancouver for the first time.

CHAPTER SEVEN

Public Space

Many of the
events held here
are celebrations
and that may be
one of the reasons
the venue is so
well-loved.

For two decades the main floor ballroom has been in demand for public and private events. Over the years, thousands of people have been welcomed into Heritage Hall. Many of the events held here are celebrations and that may be one of the reasons the venue is so well-loved by those who rent it.

Determining which events are most memorable will depend on who you ask. Many recall attending Fringe Festival performances in the nine years the building was used as a Fringe venue. Others have been to weddings, craft fairs, dances, meetings, performances, book launches, benefits, Comicon sales, memorial services or any of the other myriad events the hall has hosted.

Some of the high profile events fondly remembered include a legendary 50th birthday party held for Alma Lee (the artistic director of the Vancouver Writer's Festival) in 1990; Gloria Steinem's appearance

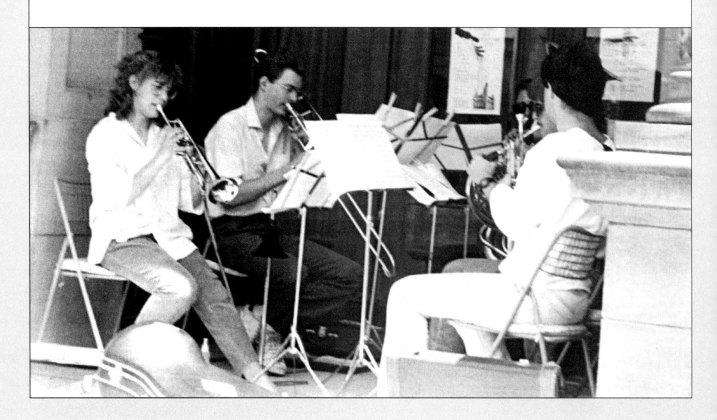

at an event sponsored by the West Coast Legal Education and Action Fund; Margaret Atwood and W.O. Mitchell's readings at a Writer's Union of Canada special gala evening in 1986; a Point in Time fashion show titled Champagne and Lace in Alice's Wonderland in 1996; Linda Lee Thomas's Tango Vivo presentation at a Vancouver Sun Community Concert in 1997; Opiate Karim, a theatrical cabaret presented by NeWorld Theatre in 2001; and Terminal City editor Jen Cressey's eclectic cabaret held for two nights in 2000.

Several groups of young musicians (and their family and friends) from the Mount Pleasant neighbourhood have occasionally rented the hall. Before these public performances, this music had mostly been heard coming from whatever garage or basement the bands used as a practice space. These alcohol-free evenings have featured such unknown but rockin' acts as My Buddy Dave.

The hall is also a favourite venue for fundraising events for local charitable organizations. Such groups as the Committee for Domestic Workers, the Spina Bifida Association, Healing Our Spirit, OutWest Performance Society, the Powell Street Festival, Vancouver Youth Theatre, the Canadian Network for International Surgery, the Philippine

Great music, fine food and dramatic speeches are just some of the many elements that bring the Public Space to life.

On Location

An episode of the TV series *Viper* transformed the main floor into a very convincing Buddhist temple.

HERITAGE HALL HAS enjoyed many incarnations in real life and has stood in for quite a few cinematic settings as well. In the last ten years the building has been used as a location for TV series, movies of the week, feature films, student productions, music videos and commercials.

Most of the film action has taken place in Gerson Hall. In recent years, set designers and art directors have used their skills to dress the room as a Buddhist Temple for *Viper*, a French police station for *Murder at the Cannes Film Festival* and an artist's studio for the *X-Files*. The room has stood in as a casino, an old-fashioned office building, a wedding hall and numerous other things. Gerson Hall was even the scene of a movie Mafia blood bath. The trompe l'œil mural had a scene of the Italian countryside placed carefully over it and fake blood ended up everywhere. (This was only allowed because the room was scheduled for repainting right after the film shoot.)

Heritage Hall is scouted far more often than it is used. It is one of a few Vancouver buildings that look original and is open to rentals. Sometimes a peek through the window is all the location scouts need to tell them the building is not going to work. But when the creative talent like what they see, they go to work with startling efficiency, and measure and make decisions in record time.

False walls, which perfectly match the room, are often built. Set decorators work magic.

Creativity and fabulous props transform the room into wondrous, believable scenes.

On shoot days, film crews come early and stay late. They arrive complete with portable power, a catering kitchen, and dressing rooms for the actors. Soon cables and lights are everywhere and windows are blacked out. Production assistants with walkie-talkies are posted at all the entrances and the whole well-oiled machine is geared towards silence whenever the word "rolling" is heard. There always seem to be twice as many people as could possibly be needed and there is a lot of standing around and waiting. Mysterious things go on all day and late into the evening and then it is all packed up and moved to the next location.

People who work in the building and those walking by are often curious about what is being shot and who the stars are. Even though the film industry has been in Vancouver for at least a decade, local people are still fascinated by the process. In exchange for renting the building as a film location, Heritage Hall coffers receive a healthy rental fee. And for a day or two the building becomes part of the illusive glamour of Hollywood North.

Women's Centre, the Electric Company Theatre Society and many, many others have hosted events here.

It has also been the site of numerous awards evenings and educational events. Sports associations, mental health organizations, cultural groups, educational institutions, environmental groups and other assorted non-profit agencies make use of the facility for special events of all kinds.

The Heritage Hall Christmas Craft Fairs are legendary. These are held for four weekends in a row starting in late November and ending just before Christmas. Heritage Hall staff and volunteers organize the fair held in the first weekend of December each year (One-of-a-Kind Christmas Craft Fair) and it has proved to be an excellent fundraising event with funds dedicated to a special project or purchase for the building. The other popular fairs are organized by Sounds and Furies (the Women's Faire) and by the local Farmer's Market Society (the Winter Market).

The longest running event at Heritage Hall is the Comicon sale held here about once a month since 1987. These events see comic book lovers of all ages and interests descend on the building to buy and sell comics and collectibles and to see their favourite comic book artists in action.

It's a place to gather and a space for celebrations.

The Haunted House Hamlet

IN THE FALL of 1988, Vancouver's Tamahnous Theatre took over the entire building for a four-and-a-half week run of *The Haunted House Hamlet*. The main hall became the chapel, Ophelia's bedroom was in the Vancouver Little Theatre basement space, and Claudius and Gertrude stalked the hallways. The audience was encouraged to move throughout the building during the performance with the way in which they moved determining how they would perceive the play. Because of this fluidity, no two people remember the play in the same way. One young man who was a high school student during this production remembers it vividly. It was his first Shakespeare experience and he says he couldn't have had a more exciting introduction to the Bard.

Roy Crowe worked at the Vancouver Volunteer Centre on the third floor and he remembers it being a little challenging to carry on day-to-day routines with the show on. "Part of this Hamlet production had a sword fight going up and down the stairs. The volunteer centre was still open and we had to phone people who had afternoon appointments and warn them they might not want to take the stairs. And of course, we could hear the battle throughout the whole building."

The Haunted House Hamlet proved to be an experience not to be forgotten for those who worked in the building, acted in the performance, or attended the show.

KEN MACDONALD PHOTOS

98

The Fringe Festival

WHEN THEATRE SPACE initiated the first annual Vancouver Fringe Festival in the Main Street/Mount Pleasant neighbourhood in September 1985, it seemed natural that Heritage Hall should figure prominently in the planning. The mid-'80s were generally an optimistic time for civic minded Vancouver residents. Local area planning was in its heyday, and people truly believed they could change their neighbourhoods in beneficial ways.

Those involved with restoring the building had always hoped the main floor and basement could serve as cultural and performance spaces. They had also hoped the revitalized building would serve as a catalyst for an overall re-awakening of Main Street itself. The organizers of the Fringe Festival also counted on bringing new life to the area. In the first year, the Fringe solicited and received support from local businesses like the IGA who staged a parking lot chicken barbeque, John's Jukes who lent a juke box for a street dance, and area merchants who offered special sidewalk sales. Heritage Hall helped with organizing and donated performance space.

It was a relationship that lasted for almost a decade. After the first year the Fringe paid a rental fee and for two weeks every September from 1985 to 1994, the resident Vancouver Little Theatre and the elegant Gerson Hall became Fringe Festival venues. The basement theatre required few adjustments to accommodate the Fringe, but Gerson Hall had to have risers and theatre lighting moved in and all the large windows blacked out. The two venues played host to scores of exciting, innovative productions over the years and thousands of Fringe-goers got to know the building. It was sad for Main Street when the Fringe left for the trendier pastures of Commercial Drive in 1995.

99

DAVID BOSWELL PHOTO

Saying "I do"

OVER THE YEARS Heritage Hall has gained a reputation as a wonderful place to have a wedding. In fact, weddings have become the most frequent special occasions celebrated in Gerson Hall. Most of those getting married are young, full of hope and, of course, in love.

Brides are especially excited at pinning down plans for the wedding. Many seem to be at last realizing dreams and fantasies they have been working on since childhood. There are those who know exactly what they want and those who bring in experts to consult – decorators, caterers, wedding planners and mothers, sisters, friends, and mothers-in-law to be.

There are a handful of men who do all the planning and a few fathers who take an active role.

The beautiful ballroom, Gerson Hall, provides the raw material around which the various fantasies come to life. Most want to make it their own with their choice of flowers, linen and lighting. Some bring in props like potted trees, garden arches, and red carpets. Most people realize the room has its own magic. With its grand scale, huge windows, stained glass chandeliers and elaborate paint, the room lets you know you are somewhere special.

As special occasions go, weddings usually come with great expectations. As a wedding venue, Heritage Hall seems to do just fine. After the event, the happy couples almost always say, "It went wonderfully. Our guests loved it. It was perfect."

Above Kurt and Namiko cut the cake, July 2001. *Left* Juniper and Lyle seal it with a kiss, October, 1999.

Another long-running event is the once-a-month Sunday afternoon social held by Together Again, a group of energetic Filipino seniors who rightfully maintain that dancing helps keep them young.

Also in the long-running renter category is Stage Door, a theatre group whose membership includes people with developmental disabilities. This agency organizes Valentine and Halloween dances at Heritage Hall. The Stage Door folks always dress up the room with hand-made decorations and rumour has it that everyone is up and dancing from the time the music starts until the last notes of the last song.

From time to time, the hall gets truly unclassifiable bookings.

From time to time, the hall gets truly unclassifiable bookings. The group of people who dressed up and role played as vampires for the evening belong in this category, as does the theatre presentation of Shakespeare's *A Midsummer Night's* (wet) *Dream* performed in the nude. The Hall is open to all possibilities. That's part of the joy of being a public facility.

WHAT'S IN A NAME?

As a title, the Main Source Management Society did not provide many clues about the society's mandate. In March, 2001, the society decided that a new, self-explanatory name was in order and it legally became the Heritage Hall Preservation Society. The society's purpose did not, however, change. It exists to restore and manage Heritage Hall, a function which hopefully will go on for many years to come.

THE VOLUNTEERS 1980 - 2002

A long and impressive list of people have helped make Heritage Hall
the fine community facility it is today.

Linda Adam
Glen Allison
Kenneth Bayfield
Wallace (Wally) Beck
Vicki Bentzen
John Bickhart
Stephanie Boggan
Connie Brill
Arthur Brock
Gail Buente
Paul Calder
Babs Capozzi
Michael Carr
Phillip Carroll
Joyce Catliff
Frank Claassen
Alistair Cook
Ellen Cornelissen
Cynthia Crampton
Duane Cromwell
Sylvia Crooks
Barbara Cupit
Dale Cuthbertson
Linda Davidson
Evelyn Davis
Diane Dieno
Bill Docksteader
Claude Douglas
Lynne Dyson
Doug Eakins
Nancy Esworthy
Georgia Evans
Gil Evans
Joyce Fitzpatrick

Linda Freer
Colin Funk
Michael Geller
Lorraine Gerard
Wolfgang Gerson
Grant Gisel
Julie Gordon
Bob Griffiths
David Griffiths
Art Guttman
Joan Haggerty
Pamela Harris
Dennis Howarth
Kari Huhtala
Barbara Jackson
Charles Keast
Perry Andrews Keith
Colleen Kelly
Shirley Kepper
Vincent Kwan
Kay Larsen
Barbara Lecky
Alma Lee
Tawney Lem
Sue Lewis
Becky Low
Michael Low
Charles Maddison
Diana Maughan
Kathleen McEvoy
Allison McGavin
Brigid McGoran
Don McKay
Nancy McKenzie

Noreen MacLeod
Heather Mersey
Stephen Mitchell
Andre Molnar
Marie Moonen
Jill Moran
Alison Morris
Pari Motamedi
Darlene Nairne
National Association of
    Watch and Clock
    Collectors (Chapter 121)
David Niederauer
Gerry O'Sullivan
Marie Pearce
Iva Pederson
Keith Pederson
Janet Percy
Helen Phillips
Andrew Pottinger
Bob Reid
Lynne Robinson
Linda Ruddy-Heisler
Joan Sandilands
Sue Sayer
Lisa Schwabe
Judy Schmitchen
Erika Scott
Peter Shrimpton
Jim Siemens
Gordon Sim
Melba Sinclair
David Shadrake
Chris Smith

Peter Smith
Andria Spindell
Peter Steele
Anne Sturrock
Stephanie Taggart
Elizabeth Telford
Maxine Thompson
Sarah Thompson
Donna Turner
Pam Vickram
Rosemary Wakefield
Anne Wallace
Sandy Walton
Peter Wardle
Aubrey Waring
Doug Warner
Maureen Webb
Jerry Wennes
Sandra Wilson
Christopher White
Sue Yates
David Young

BIBLIOGRAPHY

Davis, Chuck, ed.; *The Greater Vancouver Book,* Linkman Press, 1997.

Dominion of Canada; *Report on Public Buildings,* Sessional Papers 1916, No. 19.

Federated Association of Letter Carriers; *Convention Book of the Vancouver Branch,* no.12, published in connection with the 16th biennial convention to be held in Vancouver, B.C., Charlesworth, 1914.

Hamilton, Reuben; *Mount Pleasant Early Days,* City Archives, City Hall Vancouver, 1957.

Hyatt, Nicole; *Dominion Agricultural Building/Postal Stn. C,* unpublished student paper, UBC 1982.

Kalman, Harold, et al; *Exploring Vancouver,* UBC Press, 1978.

Kloppenborg, Niwinski, Johnson, eds.; *Vancouver: A City Album,* Douglas & McIntyre, 1991.

MacDonald, Bruce; *Vancouver, A Visual History,* Talonbooks, 1992.

Melvin, George H.; *The Post Offices of British Columbia 1858-1970,* Wayside Press, 1972.

Mills, Edward and Wright, Janet; *Agenda Paper,* Historic Sites and Monuments Board of Canada, 1982.

Modern Architecture, Vancouver, B.C., Metropolitan Press, 1911.

Plemming fonds, City of Vancouver Archives.

Public Works Canada, Pacific Region; Prospectus: Mount Pleasant Post Office, 1977.

Schwesinger, Dr. Gladys; *Recollections of Early Vancouver in my Childhood 1893-1912.* Brock Webber Print Co., 196?.

Vancouver Community College Langara Campus Journalism Dept.; *Heritage Hall: Saving Yesterday for Tomorrow,* 1985.

Vancouver Public Library Historic Building Registry (in VPL online catalogue), and all references cited in this listing.

Interviews with: Lyle Freeman, Estelle Lavine, Dr. H.K. Chin, Albert Lawrence, Reg Chase, Bill Topping, Harold Chisholm, Jean Bentley, Fred Dannells, Barry Freeman, Betty Opre, Nancy McKenzie, David Niederauer, Gil Evans, Roy Crowe, Bob Griffiths, Susan Baker, Wally Beck, David Peddle.

Langley Centennial Museum and Archives

Delta Museum and Archives

ACKNOWLEDGEMENTS

Gerry Apuada

Frank J. Baker

Susan Baker

Wally Beck

John Bell

Jean Bentley

Peter Bond

Brewery Creek
    Historical Society

Don. N. Brown

Sue Burnham

Donald Burton

Nik Burton

Reg Chase

Dr. H.K. Chen

Harold Chisholm

Frank Claassen

Cynthia Crampton

Roy Crowe

Fred Dannells

Marsha Day

Catherine Edwards

Gil Evans

Leslie Field

Michelle Frawley

Barry Freeman

Lyle Freeman

Martin Gerson

Bob Griffiths

Michelle Heinemann

Phil Hersee

Bill Hewitt

Namiko Kunimoto
    & Kurt Ellingson

Estelle Lavine

Albert Lawrence

Bruce Lindsay

Ken MacDonald

Nancy McKenzie

Betty Opre

Don Ouram

Bob Owens

David Niederauer

David Peddle

Juniper Ridington & Lyle Neff

Bill Topping

Robin Ward,
    Harbour Publishing Co.

Kate Weiss

West Coast LEAF Association

Leonard Wong

STAFF OF THE
FOLLOWING
RESOURCE AGENCIES

University of British
Columbia, Special
Collections Department

Vancouver Public Library,
Special Collections, History,
and Fine Arts Divisions

City of Vancouver Archives

British Columbia Archives

National Archives of Canada

Langley Centennial
Museum and Archives

Canadian Inventory of
Historic Buildings